Emotional Healing

Emotional Healing

Complementary Solutions for a Stress-Free Life

JAN DE VRIES

MAINSTREAM
PUBLISHING

EDINBURGH AND LONDON

First published in Great Britain in 2007 by
MAINSTREAM PUBLISHING COMPANY
(EDINBURGH) LTD
7 Albany Street
Edinburgh EH1 3UG

ISBN 9781845962715

The information in this book has been compiled by way of
general guidance in relation to the specific subjects addressed
but is not a substitute and not to be relied on for medical,
healthcare, pharmaceutical or other professional advice on specific
circumstances and in specific locations. Please consult your GP
before changing, stopping or starting any medical treatment. So far
as the author is aware, the information given is correct and up to
date as at September 2007. Practice, laws and regulations all change,
and the reader should obtain up-to-date professional advice on any
such issues. The author and publishers disclaim, as far as the law
allows, any liability arising directly or indirectly from the use, or
misuse, of the information contained in this book.

The author has made every effort to clear all copyright permissions,
but where this has not been possible and amendments are required,
the publisher will be pleased to make any necessary arrangements at
the earliest opportunity.

A catalogue record for this book is available
from the British Library.

Typeset in Garamond and Helvetica Neue

Printed and bound in Great Britain by
Cox & Wyman Ltd, Reading, Berkshire

Contents

Introduction

ONE OF the main inspirations for writing this book was a plan
that Caron Keating, the well-known broadcaster and television
presenter, and I made to record a series of programmes looking
at the many health issues that exist today relating to people's
emotions and exploring how such problems often need to be
treated in a different way.

Following an appearance that Caron and I made together on
GMTV, I clearly remember her asking if she could see me, as
she felt that there could be something seriously wrong with her.
I had a look into her eyes, using iridology, and saw indeed that
there was something present of a serious nature. I was worried
that she might have cancer, and I begged her to consult her
doctor.

Caron was a most intelligent and resolute lady who
immediately took action. She was referred to a well-known
oncologist who, after carrying out some tests, confirmed that

she had breast cancer. I saw her after the oncologist's diagnosis, as it was imperative to act quickly in an attempt to control the situation. We had a long chat and agreed how important it was that she complied completely with the oncologist's advice, but I also suggested strongly that she took immediate action regarding her diet and prescribed some supplements and herbal remedies. Luckily, Caron followed this to the letter. I recommended a lot of remedies that I am sure helped to lengthen her life by a further seven years.

After she had been ill for around three months, she returned home one day feeling particularly poorly. I went to her mother's home and stayed with her until the early hours of the morning. We had a long discussion about how people cope emotionally when they are struck by a life-threatening disease, and she asked me what could be done to help ease the worries that she and so many other women faced while in this situation. I was amazed at Caron's positivity and moved by her determination to use her own experience to help fellow sufferers. We decided that a series of television programmes on this subject would be extremely beneficial to the public and mentally started to prepare this.

On another occasion, I travelled to her home at a time when things were looking bleak. We sat in her room with the sun streaming in the window, and I glanced at her lovely children. As we talked, some tears fell, and we thought about life and how wonderful it really is. But once again we agreed that it all depends on what one makes of it, particularly when one is faced with such serious problems. Caron realised that, no matter which direction she decided to follow in her cancer treatment, a positive attitude would help with whatever healing methods were made available to her. Both of us agreed that where there was a will there was a way, and in this way we continued to optimistically tackle the difficulties that afflicted Caron's health.

As she explained so well during that visit, the body does not really want to be ill, but sometimes there are too many circumstances that affect people's health, and our system cannot cope. At the end of the day, we all have a responsibility to decide what to do about it. Caron bravely fought an enormous battle and looked positively at what could be done. Every time a new problem occurred, she tackled it with great courage.

Finally, however, Caron could fight no more and on Tuesday, 13 April 2004, she died at her mother's home in Kent, surrounded by her family. In a statement by her family, they said that she had conducted her battle against cancer 'with enormous courage, tenacity and optimism'. Sir Cliff Richard, a family friend, said, 'Caron was gifted, talented, wonderful with people and, to crown it all, she was beautiful and courageous to the end.' I could not agree more.

The courage exhibited by this remarkable young woman during our many visits together has encouraged me greatly over the years. I often think of the times when we worked together, and the programmes that we planned together have been the inspiration for this book.

ONE

Stress

LEVELS OF stress and anxiety have reached epidemic proportions, and there can be no doubt that this represents a huge problem in modern society. Indeed, for most of us stress and anxiety have become an inescapable part of our everyday existence, and in some cases this is literally ruining people's lives. Whatever the cause – a hard day at the office, screaming children, the journey home, the never-ending list of things to do – stress causes both emotional and physical problems as well as impairing our ability to enjoy life to the fullest.

I recently attended a lecture given by a psychiatrist on this subject, and he went as far as to say that 95 per cent of stress results from our modern lifestyles. At work, as companies downsize and corporate competition intensifies, everyone is putting in longer hours, but job security is a constant worry, and the threat of unemployment haunts many people. Technology may have eliminated many tedious, mind-numbing tasks, but it has also led to increased pressure for an instant response, and the cumulative effect is that people are arriving home from the office overstressed and irritable after a long day. As more and more women now work full time, people have increasing concerns about balancing their work and home life, and even today's children lead high-pressured lives. All of this can have a detrimental effect on family relationships, leading to unhappiness, separation and even divorce.

To be honest, life without stress can be very boring, and a certain amount of positive stress can be beneficial. But when the situation becomes so bad that it affects us in every way possible, then we have to address it by trying to find out what aspect of our life is detrimentally affecting our health.

WHY IS STRESS BAD FOR YOU AND WHAT DOES IT DO TO YOUR BODY?

When stress emerges, the whole body starts an alarm reaction. Most people are familiar with the body's dramatic response to an emergency. The heart pounds, the muscles contract and the lungs expand, and while this is happening we are capable of greater than normal strength and speed. This response is the body's way of enabling us to rescue ourselves when faced with an emergency. We don't have to think about it to make it happen – it's automatic.

The same physical reaction occurs in what is sometimes called a chronic stress response. In this instance, stress is a psychological and physical response to the demands of daily life that exceed a person's ability to cope successfully. Whether we are stuck in traffic, about to give a speech in front of a group, sitting in the doctor's waiting room or worrying about whether we are about to lose our jobs, the human stress response happens automatically. The difference between the two is that the body's response in an emergency starts and resolves itself quickly. The response to the threat of losing one's job might not.

In an emergency situation, the adrenal glands (located above the kidneys) secrete the hormone cortisol until the emergency passes. Then the body returns to its normal function. However, chronic stress is more complex and can last longer. When our body is subjected to high levels of cortisol for an extended time, our health can be damaged. Studies have shown that increased cortisol production caused by long-term chronic stress may damage the entire nervous system and suppress the immune system.

There is ample evidence that living a highly stressful lifestyle damages the heart, raises blood pressure and can contribute to digestive problems. Not surprisingly, stress can also be damaging to the brain, even leading to premature brain cell ageing. Stress can also lead to a breakdown of tissue, influencing bones, muscles and nerves, and can cause much toxicity in the body.

Tension caused by stress can also cause problems, though it is interesting to note initially that tension is actually a natural state of being. It is a most important factor in physical life and is responsible for controlling the harmonious distribution of energy through the body. Call it life, health or what you will, it is the factor that prevents molecules from flying into space. However, tension as we know it is muscular in nature, and when it is persistently present it can actually precipitate soluble calcium from the bloodstream into the joints. The results of this can include rheumatism, lumbago and other similar afflictions.

When we consider the three bodies of man – namely the physical, mental and emotional – it quickly becomes obvious how detrimental stress can be as we get trapped in a vicious circle. There can be many triggers for emotional stress, including work resentment, jealousy, emotional upset, unhappy marriages, anxieties, worries, depression, irritability, moodiness, lack of enjoyment in life, loneliness – a lot of the problems that I have written about in this book. Physically, this can result in symptoms such as weakness, dizziness, trembling, cramps, muscle tensions, high blood pressure, restlessness, headaches, insomnia, lack of energy, dry mouth, butterflies in the stomach and ringing in the ears. It can also lead to more serious problems like compulsive behaviour, alcohol abuse, drug use, smoking, addictions, aggressiveness, overworking, short-temperedness and impatience . . . the list goes on and on. Mentally, we very often see that stress can lead to memory problems, being critical, getting things out of proportion, distorted ideas and attitude problems, and this can affect our health with migraines, headaches, irritable bowel syndrome, ulcers, heart attacks, angina, asthma, skin problems, lowering of the immune system, stomach disorders and peptic, duodenal or gastric ulcers.

Thus we see that not only does stress affect the body mechanically, but also mentally and emotionally, and this is when the situation becomes a catch-22, with stress begetting stress. The result is the enormous increase that we have seen in cases of cancer, degenerative diseases, ME, osteoporosis, post-viral syndrome and so on.

During my career I have witnessed the effects that long-term stress can have on people and nowhere has this been more obvious than in Northern Ireland and the Irish Republic. I have carried out a lot of work in Belfast and admire the Irish people immensely. But during the years that I have worked there, it has been impossible to ignore the reality that rates of degenerative disease and other illnesses have increased, and I believe that this is due to the great stress that the people there have endured throughout the Troubles. I have seen a similar situation in Dublin, where the swift growth of the economy may have brought a lot of wealth but has also put people under negative stress as they struggle to cope with these rapid developments. It is 40 years since I first lectured in the Republic of Ireland at Trinity College. When I visit the area today, I see the consequences of the terrific problems that have arisen there.

Stress-related problems range from the mild to the severe and, in some cases, the fuse can blow and psychosis and neurosis can then become a possibility. For some people, anxiety and stress are persistent and overwhelming, and can interfere with daily life. A disorder called generalised anxiety disorder can cause its sufferers to worry constantly, always expect the worst to happen and feel tense all of the time. Sufferers cannot just 'snap out of it' because this disorder is caused by an imbalance of chemicals in the brain.

The good news is that alterations in the central nervous

system and the immune system can be reversed when stress is removed. The key is to learn how to deal with daily stress to allow the body to return to its normal state. We have to look not only at our physical state but also our mental and emotional states, and then find the right balance.

WHAT ARE SOME CONVENTIONAL TREATMENTS FOR ANXIETY AND STRESS?

Antidepressants and anti-anxiety medications are frequently used in combination with behavioural therapy to ease anxiety and stress. The two major classes of antidepressants are selective serotonin reuptake inhibitors (SSRIs) and tricyclic antidepressants (TCAs). These medications work by inhibiting the reuptake of neurotransmitters such as serotonin, resulting in the accumulation of these neurotransmitters. Brain chemicals such as serotonin are thought to be low in conditions such as anxiety and depression. Preventing their reuptake by the nerve cells essentially increases the amount of available chemical.

Anti-anxiety medications include the benzodiazepines. These can relieve symptoms within a short time. These medications belong to the group of medicines called central nervous system (CNS) depressants (medicines that slow down the nervous system).

Although such antidepressant medication can help, as described, to regulate the brain's neurotransmitters and help relieve the symptoms of depression and stress, these medications can also cause a number of side effects, such as nausea, sedation, weight gain and sexual problems (decreased libido, delayed orgasm or erectile dysfunction). Other side effects include drowsiness, loss of coordination, fatigue and mental confusion. These effects make it dangerous for people taking benzodiazepines to drive or operate some machinery. In addition, many anti-anxiety medications may be habit-forming, causing mental or physical dependence, especially when taken for a long time or in high doses. Benzodiazepines can also cause seizures if abruptly discontinued.

SO WHAT IS THE ALTERNATIVE?

As an alternative to antidepressants, a natural substance that has been found to have a similar effect on the body is *L-theanine*. Since ancient times, it has been said that drinking green tea brings relaxation. The substance that is responsible for this sense of relaxation is *L-theanine*. *L-theanine* has been shown to promote deep muscle relaxation and improve good-quality sleep. Since it does not cause sedation, it can be taken during the day to alleviate stress and anxiety.

Although it is not fully understood how *L-theanine* works, scientists believe that it supports the balance of various neurotransmitters in the brain. In a laboratory study, researchers found that it is able to cross the blood–brain barrier to support the activity of certain neurotransmitters. In a recent test, the brain activity of 50 volunteers was measured after the oral administration of 50 to 200mg of *L-theanine*. It promoted the generation of alpha brainwaves, considered to be an index of relaxation, in the volunteers. This study concluded that one way in which *L-theanine* promotes relaxation in humans is by increasing alpha brainwaves.

L-theanine has also been shown to help the regulation of blood pressure. The same neurotransmitters that help us relax also regulate blood pressure in our bodies, and the absorption of *L-theanine* results in slightly lowered blood pressure. Laboratory studies have demonstrated that it affects both the nervous system and the cardiovascular system. Thus, its calming effect on our mental state is augmented by lowering blood pressure as well. However, in these tests the blood pressure was never lowered to abnormally low levels.

Using an *L-theanine* supplement is a safe alternative because it will relieve anxiety and promote relaxation without causing the daytime sedation and grogginess that is associated with prescription medications on the market today. Recommendations for *L-Theanine* are one UltraCaps two or three times daily. If additional support is desired, this can be increased to two UltraCaps three times daily. If pregnant, breast-feeding or taking prescription drugs, you should consult your health practitioner prior to taking this supplement.

The nervous system controls and integrates all the activities of the body – not only on a physical level but also psychologically. The system may become debilitated and fatigued through factors such as stress, shock and faulty nutrition. In these circumstances, a nerve tonic plays a useful role, strengthening, feeding and revitalising the system.

I always find *Avena sativa* from Alfred Vogel to be one of the best tonics for stress. *Avena sativa* is a traditional herbal nerve tonic made from fresh oat seeds. It is similar to having porridge in the morning, which helps greatly to reduce stress, but is so much simpler to take and will be of tremendous benefit in any stressful situation. It is known to have a nutritive and restorative action on the nervous system and also has mild sedative properties.

Avena sativa contains high amounts of vitamin B, minerals and other nutrients necessary for the proper functioning of the nervous system. These constituents probably account for its 'restorative' effects in the treatment of anxiety, debility and exhaustion. It also contains indole alkaloids, the most active of which is known as gramine. These have been shown to relax smooth muscle and exert a sedative action on the nervous system. It is also of benefit to those suffering from insomnia. Research carried out by two Edinburgh physicians using electroencephalogram (EEG) to assess sleep quality has shown that those using *Avena sativa* had a quieter sleep than those in the control group.

As *Avena sativa* is such a mild sedative, it may even be used to calm children who are upset and has been used successfully for the clinical treatment of hyperactivity in children – though this is not an alternative to implementing necessary dietary changes. It has also been used to help with symptoms of withdrawal when treating addiction. Ayurvedic physicians also used oats to help with opium withdrawal.

Adults should take 20 drops, 2 or 3 times a day, before meals, and children should be given 1 drop per year of age (2–12 years) in a little water, 2 or 3 times a day. It can be administered long term and has no known restrictions. However, it is not recommended for pregnant and nursing women unless directed by a healthcare professional.

When stress results in a lack of energy, then *Ginsavena* can be of great help. *Ginsavena* is a combination of energising and calming herbs used to strengthen and fortify the nerves. It contains both energising *Eleutherococcus senticosus* (Siberian ginseng) and *Avena sativa*.

It is very common nowadays to see conditions of exhaustion and debility alongside anxiety and nervous tension. Treating just one side of this problem is not sufficient. Increasing energy without calming the central nervous system may well make matters worse. The energy produced is nervous energy that further drains the adrenal glands.

Eleutherococcus supports the metabolic processes of the body and has a revitalising effect, helping to increase energy levels that may have been depleted due to stress. It is also known as the 'female' ginseng and is often recommended to women going through the menopause, as it has a balancing effect on female hormones. The *Avena sativa* content, as described above, has a calming effect, so *Ginsavena*'s combination of herbs thus deals with both the restlessness and listlessness that can result from situations such as bereavement, divorce and moving house.

This remedy is only recommended for adults and should be taken at the dose of 20 drops, twice a day, in a little water. It has no restrictions for long-term use. However, if it is needed for longer than two months, a two-week break is recommended. Those who suffer from diabetes, schizophrenia, heart disease or high blood pressure should consult a healthcare professional before using *Ginsavena*, as should those taking the Pill or HRT.

Products containing *Eleutherococcus* should not be taken with caffeine. Take it at a different time of day to vitamin B and C supplements, as it aids their secretion. It is not recommended for pregnant or nursing women unless directed by a healthcare professional.

With any stress condition, it is crucial that one gets plenty of restful sleep, as well as carrying out relaxation exercises. But due to the hectic pace of life today, many people have problems with insomnia, nervous tension and disturbed sleep patterns. There are several herbal remedies that can be used to help resolve these problems, and they do not have the negative side effects associated with many modern pharmaceutical drugs.

Valerian-Hops Complex combines the sedative properties of *Valeriana officinalis* (Valerian) and *Humulus lupulus* (Hops). Valerian grows widely throughout Europe and the root of this plant has been used in herbal remedies for many centuries. Hops are climbing plants that can be found in swamps and hedges. Being an important ingredient in beer, they are now extensively cultivated for commercial purposes.

These ingredients are beneficial as a sedative and relaxant. Valerian acts as a herbal tranquilliser and is widely recommended for those with nervous excitement and disturbed sleep patterns. The relaxing properties are due to the valepotriates and volatile oils present (especially valerenal and valerenic acid). Valerenic acid inhibits the breakdown of the neurotransmitter gamma-amino-butyric acid (GABA), increasing its concentration. This then leads to a decrease in central nervous system activity.

Hops contain humulones and lupulones, which are metabolised in the body to form a compound known as 2-methyl-3-buten-2-ol, which exerts a sedative effect on the central nervous system, making them a useful treatment for restlessness, over-excitability, anxiety, tension and sleep problems. They are also an antispasmodic bitter, enhancing digestion and easing intestinal tension.

Adults should take between 20 and 30 drops in a little water, half an hour before retiring. Children should take 1 drop per year of age (2–12 years) in a little water or juice half an hour before bedtime. This product can safely be used to treat hyperactivity (put drops in fruit juice if needed). There are no restrictions on long-term use. This preparation should not be used to replace prescribed tranquillisers without consulting a healthcare professional. It may, however, be used as an adjunct to such treatment. It may be used for both acute and chronic disorders. It is not recommended for pregnant and nursing women unless directed by a healthcare professional.

Such remedies are of tremendous help. However, I also find that some amino acids, vitamins, minerals and trace elements give us the necessary relaxation which is important.

In situations where stress leads to violence, then the homoeopathic remedy *Staphysagria* will be beneficial.

In addition to taking these remedies, there are a lot of things that we can do to overcome stress and to reduce tension, for instance:

1. Take a physical break – exercise, walk or otherwise interrupt your routine for five minutes or so at regular intervals throughout the working day.

2. Do not cheat on sleep – try not to work at home, but, if you must, stop at least an hour before you go to bed. Develop a hobby to take your mind off the job.

3. Learn to recognise stress – watch for indicators like increased smoking, additional drinking and frequently disturbed sleep.

4. Stay with a problem – do not switch to something else and leave it unsolved. Step back and reflect on it objectively before pursuing a conclusion.

5. Clarify your personal values – recognise when it pays to fight and when it pays to yield.

6. Face up to your tensions – accept the fact that you have them and work at ways to reduce them. This will help reduce organic effects.

7. Plan happy times with your family – do things together that could provide you all with happy memories. Your husband or wife deserves the same consideration. Call home regularly when you're away on a trip, especially in the mornings.

This is a good start, and if you want to de-stress your life, I can wholeheartedly recommend the Hara breathing method. Have a good stretch, think positively, get plenty of sleep, take physical exercise and enjoy yourself. At several times during the day, do some breathing exercises. This will help to cleanse as well as strengthen the body.

- *Find a quiet place to sit down, with the back as straight as possible*
- *Rest the left wrist on the right knee*
- *Close the eyes and inhale normally*
- *Close the right nostril with the right thumb, inhaling fully*
- *Pause and exhale to the count of two*
- *Block the left nostril using the little finger*
- *Inhale and hold the breath to the count of ten*
- *Release the thumb and exhale fully through the right nostril*
- *Count to five*
- *Keeping the left nostril closed, inhale through the right nostril to the count of two*
- *Close both nostrils and count to eight*
- *Release the left nostril, exhale and count to five*

A good selection of relaxation exercises can be found in my book *Body Energy*.

Also make sure that you keep to a stress-free diet. A diet that is high in animal protein can exacerbate stress and sometimes can even be disastrous, leading to outbursts of nervous tension. It is also important that, because stress can often cause a breakdown of tissue, people who suffer from stress consume good carbohydrates, not white flour or sugar. More advice can be found in my book *Nature's Gift of Food*.

To summarise, my recommendations for dealing with the stresses of modern life are as follows: first, the most important thing is to recognise stress; second, follow a low-stress diet, which I have advocated in my books on food; third, try relaxation, such as the Hara breathing exercise which I have also mentioned in many of my books; and, fourth, take some homoeopathic or herbal remedies specifically formulated for stressful situations.

The final suggestion I would make is to maintain a positive attitude. This is vital in all stages of life and particularly when things are getting on top of us. As people get older and reach retirement age, I often hear them saying, 'I am getting old: that is why I am retiring.' When people no longer feel that they can lead a useful life, this can lead to a degeneration of their mental state and then their health. It is interesting to see that when positive action is taken, one gets a positive reaction.

I greatly admire Dr Claire Weekes, who has done much to show people suffering from nervous illness how to help themselves and recover. In the first chapter of her book *Self-Help for Your Nerves*, she speaks about sensitisation – the simple cause of so much nervous illness – and shows clearly how some nervous reactions can be balanced. She remarks how patients can be constantly worried and harbour negative thoughts about the future, but when they start to pick up and find the courage to get on with life, then their health goes from strength to strength.

A 20-year-old girl who came to see me with multiple sclerosis was understandably depressed. She had a lot of stress to deal with, her boyfriend mistreated her and her head hung low. I had to give this young girl a very strong remedy, *Nerve Factors* from Michael's, which lifted her spirits. I then said to her that she still had two hands to write, she was still beautiful and there was still a lot of good work for her to do. That little talk made her take note, and she picked herself up again. She realised that life was indeed worthwhile and has now gone on to write a successful book.

TWO

Fear

A NUMBER of weeks ago, I stood before an audience of a few hundred people to give a lecture. When there are so many people in attendance, I usually ask them to write down any questions they would like to put to me, and I try to answer as many of these as possible during the break.

I had to think deeply when one person wrote: 'Fear is dominating my life. I am preoccupied as I am constantly trying to analyse why I feel edgy, tense and afraid. Why am I so afraid of something I cannot even identify? What is preventing me from living life free from fear?'

At times, fear can be a positive force in our lives. It can force us to pay attention in a potentially dangerous situation, for example when crossing a busy road. Negative fears, however, can lead to an enormous amount of problems. In Holland, we have a saying, 'People are suffering from the things that they fear.' They have greater burdens on their shoulders than God gave them to carry. We can be ruled by fear in our workplace, fear of the unknown, fear for oneself and even fear of fear. The worst of all these is a fear of fear, which I later discovered was what that particular question was all about.

As there was insufficient time to devote to such a complex issue during the break, I asked this lady if she could see me afterwards so that I could give her a deeper explanation of what fear is, what causes it and how it can be overcome. Following our initial talk, I saw this patient again in my clinic several times to offer her help and support. She was distraught about this fear, which was ruling her life. Strange as it may seem, it surfaced at a time in her life when she was happy and had no particular problems. Everything was going so well that she got it into her head that something would happen to destroy her happiness, and she then blew this worry out of all proportion. After a while, she was harbouring so much fear that it became a negative factor, affecting her mentally, physically and emotionally, and causing her immense disquiet.

Thankfully, I was able to help this patient through counselling, acupuncture and the prescription of some remedies, but for other sufferers this kind of negative fear can lead to anxiety, phobias, accidents and obsessive disorders – in fact, all sorts of problems that can stand in the way of a person leading a normal, healthy life. The best way of dealing with a fear of the unknown is to focus one's mind on positive thoughts. If we only look inwards, we can become upset and fearful about many factors, such as health, work, relationships and so on. Instead, we need to look outside ourselves, look afresh at the future and make a decision about what we can do to improve our lives. We can lose out on such a lot through fearful thoughts and feelings, but our lives can be transformed by replacing this negativity with more positive and rational thinking. And this was the case for another of my young patients.

One of the diagnostic techniques I use with patients is iridology. An experienced iridologist can discover a lot about someone's physical and mental health by looking into the eyes. The eyes are the windows to the soul, as the Old Book says, but they can also reveal a lot about the condition that a patient is in. When I looked into this young girl's eyes, I got a shock, as I saw that she was harbouring a fear beyond explanation.

My readers will no doubt be asking themselves, 'What do you actually see when you look into a patient's eyes?' Iridology is a study of the iris of the eye. It is a safe, non-invasive diagnostic science and a practice that can reveal such things as inflammation and the general state of a person's health. It provides invaluable information when one is trying to establish the root causes of ailments, revealing what treatment is required. Nature provides us with, shall we say, a 'television screen' that shows us not only the reflexes of the body but also nerve fibres. Research work being carried out into iridology offers a scientific explanation of how it works precisely, and it is encouraging to learn, through this research, how the iris reveals one's individual strengths and weaknesses, and also where correction is needed to rectify a situation.

This poor girl's eyes showed a lot of problems in her circulatory system, her digestive system, her eliminatory system and her respiratory system. While at first glance she appeared to be in reasonably good health, her nervous system was in fact in a chronic condition and showed some signs of degeneration. When I asked her what unpleasant incidents she had been through during her life, I could hardly believe it. She had been raped several times, which had caused her a lot of psychological problems. She had contracted childhood illnesses that were not properly treated, and then, when she reached adulthood, her mind was so full of fear, worrying that yet another problem would surface in her life, that she felt totally helpless. Life, as we know in iridology, goes through cycles – sometimes positive, sometimes negative – but when the majority of these cycles are negative, one can uncover a great deal through examining the iris.

She was intrigued by what I had discovered about her through iridology, and perhaps this made her wonder if I was some sort of clairvoyant, which I certainly am not. I told her scientifically where her problems lay through looking into the irises of her eyes, and I realised that a lot had to be corrected in this young lady. Her constitution was weak, and I could see that she had become completely worn down by the turmoil she had endured during her life. Several lesions showed up in the eyes, she had lymphatic congestion, her eyes were very irritated, her digestive system was definitely disturbed and the tension in her pupils showed that she had little resistance and was extremely unhappy. Because of her circumstances, she had become quite isolated. She paid very little attention to the food that she ate, and so her dietary management was extremely poor, which led to further problems. Basically, she had lost all interest in life and in herself, but, worse than that, she also exhibited a fear of herself and fear of life in general. In tears, she told me that she could make very little sense of life and asked if I could help her to pick up the pieces.

I wondered what I could do to help this unfortunate human being and decided that my first step would have to be to build up her confidence so that she could start to believe in herself and feel thankful that she still had two arms, two legs and a pair of beautiful eyes. She needed to believe that her life would improve if she became more positive. But this was very difficult, as she felt completely unloved and had been so badly treated that she no longer trusted anyone.

She was an intelligent girl, because when I said to her, 'We have to do something, and when you become well again, you will be able to help other people, because then you will have empathy for their problems and will learn to love your neighbour as yourself', she gave a very wise response: 'Well, I do not love myself, so how can I show my love to others?' I explained that when we are able to love and care for ourselves as we should, then we are also able to share that love with others. We invariably lose sight of the fact that we are born in love and that love surrounds us in so many ways. Love is the greatest form of happiness. To show love towards others can be tremendously beneficial both to them and to ourselves. When we make the effort to boost our own happiness by clearing our mind of negative feelings and replacing these with positive ones, with the right love for ourselves and for others, life will then be beautiful.

In an attempt to help her, I gave this girl a job to do involving children, which she took on. However, after a trial period, she came back to me and said she was sitting in a valley of tears.

'What can I do to get rid of these miserable feelings? I feel so inadequate and hopeless towards others. You talk to me about being positive, but how can I be positive when I am still surrounded by all these fears?'

I explained that her fears would not disappear overnight, just as they did not appear overnight. It all takes time, and I continued to offer her encouragement. Today, that same girl is one of the finest practitioners of aromatherapy and reflexology in this country. I am greatly encouraged when I witness how successful such cases are when patients follow my advice and are able to replace negative thoughts with positive ones.

On another occasion, a lady said to me that she was so fearful about a specific situation that it had taken over her whole life. I could see that this fear had made her become selfish, as she constantly dwelled on her own problems without thinking of the effect her behaviour had on those around her. In order to help calm her fears, I prescribed *Emergency Essence* and *Centaurium*, both of which are brilliant. I also gave her a course of acupuncture, which gave her a lot of extra help. Over the course of her treatment, I spoke to her in depth about the benefits of sharing her life with others. Eventually, she was able to respond positively and told me that she was thinking about becoming a counsellor in order to help other people who were going through difficult times. In sharing her life with others, she regained so much positivity that all the fears in her life were eventually overcome.

Thus we can see that through helping others we help ourselves, and I was reminded of this recently when I wasn't feeling very well one day. This seldom happens, as God has gifted me with a tremendous strength, but on this occasion I was concerned that I was probably not in the correct frame of mind to carry out a lecture that had been arranged, and I was afraid that I would be a let-down to the people who had travelled to see me. But as the minutes ticked by, people I had known for years started to flood in to the lecture hall. I knew of their struggles and how they had overcome them. I saw their smiles as they sat down. One person who had even written some poetry on his recovery was sitting in the audience.

I still did not feel very well, but when one particular lady came in I thought back to the time she consulted me years earlier when I practised in Harley Street. She looked extremely well and so happy now, but it had been a totally different story all those years ago when she showed me some letters from her oncologist stating that she had only a month to live. She was terribly afraid, and I was aware from experience that, in some cases, cancer patients can be so scared about the future and where it will lead that they make themselves more and more ill. As I say to all of them, the mind is stronger than the body, but in order to influence the body positively we need to tell ourselves in a constructive way that we will get better.

When I looked at her situation, I was also worried that this lady would never make it. However, I picked myself up and became positive, and, in an encouraging voice, I advised her what she needed to do. She followed my instructions to the letter and was obedient in doing whatever I asked of her. I also told her to be positive and to dismiss any negativity she encountered when she was told that her time was short and she had to put her affairs in order. There she was now, sitting among the spectators, blooming and happy, and she stood up to tell the audience how she had consulted me all those years earlier when she had been given just one month to live. Now, 16 years later, she said, 'Today, I am here in your audience and my cancer has gone.' She never had another day's illness after she overcame that trauma. Is there a possibility that we can overcome cancer through our thoughts and positive thinking? Indeed there is – as I have witnessed first hand in my own family. There we see again that the mind is stronger than the body.

On this particular day, through thinking back to the time when she was so ill and how she had overcome it, this former patient had now healed me and given me the strength to proceed with the lecture. A friend whom I had known for many years, who lectured at Cambridge University, came up to me afterwards and said, 'That was the best lecture you have ever given, Jan.' I was so happy to see how we human beings can help and support one another, sharing positive thoughts and helping each other to heal. When we are faced with fears, we often wonder whether or not we will make it through to the other side. But the power of positive thinking, about which I have written so much, was reinforced in a very personal way at that lecture, and I was proof that one can do it. Not only does this benefit others but it also brings benefit to oneself.

As the Old Book, the Bible, says, there is no fear in love. When we show love to others, we are often rewarded by its reciprocation. Feeling loved can help us cope and overcome our fears. There is a place for real communication in our day-to-day lives at home and at work. Sometimes words are not always required, but providing support to the individual through friendship is something that often helps those suffering from fear. Friendship gives more meaning to life, and if the person whose mind is in turmoil senses that there is a real love and understanding for their problem, and if they accept this support willingly, then that will indeed make life a lot happier.

Dr Bach remedies such as *Rock Rose* are often of great help to those suffering from fear. Of my own flower remedies, *Confidence Essence* has been of tremendous help to many people, while *Agrimony*, the liver herb, is also a wonderful remedy.

There are so many things that one can do to help oneself when faced with fear – the most important being to develop a positive attitude. If we can face the future with a more positive outlook, then we won't encounter fear. Fear can be overcome, and when replaced by love this will carry us through our lifetime.

THREE

Grief

GRIEF IS described in the dictionary as 'sorrow; distress; great mourning'. Such feelings commonly result from the loss of a loved one but can also be caused by separation or divorce, when one partner finds the situation difficult to overcome and has to go through a healing process. A person experiencing this kind of emotional trauma is vulnerable to a long list of health problems and associated symptoms, including digestive problems and degenerative illnesses.

I clearly remember one lady who could not get over the loss of her husband some years earlier. Her grief had affected her health so much that she could not eat and almost became anorexic. This was not only because she loved him so much but also because she could not accept the fact that he had gone.

I was very touched by this lady, because I could see that she had really suffered through not being able to express the grief and sorrow she felt over her loss. We see this often when grief is suppressed. Shakespeare said it so well, 'Give sorrow words: the grief that does not speak, whispers the o'er-fraught heart and bids it break.' If only some people would give themselves permission to break down and accept the loss instead of grieving silently, then things might become less painful for them to accept. This lady's health was so badly affected that her mind had also become confused, but thankfully I was able to help through a combination of remedies and counselling.

When talking to the recently bereaved, showing a lot of love and understanding will help immensely. In such circumstances, showing sympathy is a positive act and this will provide much comfort to a mourner. But words of sympathy must be chosen very carefully. There are many kinds of grief and bereavement, and different people cope in different ways. There are also different ways to find comfort or sympathy, and one should never underestimate the tremendous help that can be obtained from a good listener.

On another occasion, a young mother brought her little baby daughter to me. The little girl was suffering from uncontrollable fits, and, although she was on the strongest drugs, nothing had really helped. This woman was in tears as she sat before me, having been told that her baby had no chance of survival, and, yet, with a small cranial adjustment, she did survive. When I met the mother recently, she told me what an excellent pupil her daughter was at school. The fits had completely gone since I carried out the cranial adjustment. She was growing up well and was a blessing to her mother. Nevertheless, the woman told me that after receiving the initial diagnosis she had gone through a period of grief at the thought of losing her baby, and this had caused her a lot of stress.

Grief is something that we have to resign ourselves to. It is so difficult, but relief from the mental and emotional stresses of grief can often be gained by taking some homoeopathic remedies or by having acupuncture treatment, which I often give in such circumstances. One of the finest remedies available for emotional upset or grief at the loss of a loved one, and one which has never disappointed me, is *Ignatia*. This remedy, taken twice a day at a dosage of 10 or even 15 drops, will often work wonders. I also find that tissue salts, like *Natrium Mur*, and nerve tonics like *Avena sativa* can help a lot in overcoming the terrible feelings of grief, especially when a partnership comes to an end and the one who is left behind endures deep loneliness and emptiness. When grief is overcome, we will be able to find happiness in this life again and appreciate what life can still hold for us.

Death is not easy to accept, as it is final. But it is something that none of us can escape. It comes to us all sooner or later. Long ago, when someone died, the body was quickly transported away and was not seen. Everyone tried to avoid thinking about death. However, as this is something that will affect us all, it might be more helpful to accept the inevitable and change our way of thinking. We could learn to look at death as a new beginning, because we do know that death is not the end.

Shortly before he died, one of my best friends had a sort of revelation. He said, 'When you go to sleep, you don't know for how long you are going to sleep – it might be an hour, but even if it is for days or months or years, you are still asleep.' He felt sure that when his sleep finished, a new life would be waiting for him. This belief, traditionally and through the generations, has been of immense comfort to so many.

One person who devoted her life to changing the way we think about death was Elisabeth Kübler Ross. In 1945, as a member of the International Voluntary Service for Peace, she visited the Nazi concentration camp, Majdanek, where tens of thousands of Jewish prisoners were gassed to death. In the cells where the prisoners spent their final hours, she found butterflies carved into the walls, and this for her became symbolic of the amazing transformation that she came to believe occurred when people died. While the people who made those carvings did not know exactly what fate was about to befall them, these butterflies represented their belief in freedom.

This experience affected Kübler Ross deeply, and she spent her life challenging the Western world's attitude to death and teaching people how to accept it. After going to work in America, she was horrified by the way that terminally ill patients were treated in hospital and realised the importance of spending time with people who are dying and allowing them the opportunity to recognise they are at the end of their life and to talk about it instead of denying it. In her most famous book, *On Death and Dying*, she described the five phases that she believed people go through when they find out they are going to die: denial, anger, bargaining, depression and acceptance, and these have now also been recognised as stages often experienced by those who are grieving for loved ones.

My father was instrumental in forming my attitude towards death and grief. A lot of people have asked me why I did not grieve for my father or mother and yet I grieved for my Samoyed dog for quite a few months. The simple reason is that common sense prevailed. Following imprisonment by the Nazis during the Second World War, my father was barely alive when he returned home, and we all felt that he would not have long to live. When we asked him about the terrible ordeal he had gone through, he said that it wasn't the physically strong who coped with being tortured by the Germans, it was the spiritually strong. That is how we should look at death. Although it is not always easy, we have to be strong in spirit to accept it when it comes to us. There are some cycles in life that prepare us for death, and I believe that deep down in everybody's hearts there is an acceptance of death: we know that we cannot run away from it.

Nearing the end, my father looked back over his life and told us of the privileges he had had, and, although he suffered before he went, he knew he was going to a place that was far brighter and far better than the one he was leaving behind. He was happy to go, and he asked us all, 'Are you not happy that I am going so that I will at last be free of all this suffering?' Although we want to keep the ones we love here with us, sometimes they are actually content to go. If that is their wish, then it is better to accept it and let them go from this earthly scene to somewhere that is far better.

In my mother's case, I knew that her life was coming to an end when she slowly lost her memory. Although she was quite happy in herself, one could see that deep down she was no longer here and was looking forward to another life to come. So, although I was heartbroken at the loss of both of my parents, my mind was at peace as they both had great hope for the future.

So, why then did I grieve for several months for my dog whose life ended suddenly? Although she had had a good quality of life, her health deteriorated quickly when both her liver and kidneys failed. I said goodbye to her as usual on leaving for work in the morning, but in hindsight I realise I should have stayed with her. However, I went back to see her before the vet came to end her life. In all her suffering and in all her pain, when I went to comfort her one last time, she used the last of her strength to give me her paw to thank me for all I had done for her. That gesture of friendship, indicating the love that there was between us, nearly destroyed me, and every time I think about it I still feel broken-hearted that I lost her at a time when she showed such a desire in her eyes to stay here and yet she knew that her life was coming to an end.

Similarly, I once became quite depressed when I lost six people I loved in the course of just one year. This certainly shook me, but I then said to myself, 'How many new lives are brought into this world every day?' After pondering, I accepted that we should be grateful for the eternal circle of life.

Something that can be of immense help to those reaching the end of their days is to calmly meditate on their life and to pray, with thankfulness, that their life meant so much to them and then to wait until they are reunited with their loved ones again.

Isn't it wonderful that there is hope for a life to come? When you blow out a candle, the smoke still goes up into the cosmos – that shows that the spirit doesn't die and that there is hope for a new life. Mother Teresa and Princess Diana died at around the same time. When I was asked to comment on their lives on a radio programme, I likened Mother Teresa's long life to a candle that slowly burned. When the candle went out, the smoke from it was drawn into the atmosphere. That was a symbol of the many good works she did for others and showed that her spirit was still alive. Princess Diana also had a great love for people, but her candle was extinguished too soon. However, the smoke from her candle still rose into the air as a sign that her spirit lives on in the good work she had become involved in and which is continuing around the world today. When grieving, that is the hope that we have – when this earthly body dies, the spirit will be kept alive.

Life is sometimes very strange and wonderful, and we often see that the spirit of the person who has gone can be of great help to those grieving. It reminds us to live our lives to the full and then, when we have done all that we can, enables us to look forward to going on to a better place.

As I have said, death is not easy to accept, but if you have loved and you receive love from someone, then one day all this sorrow will come to an end.

FOUR

Guilt

I HAVE seen many patients in my lifetime who have felt guilty about one thing or another and this can lead to problems with anxiety, insecurity and lack of confidence. The other day, for example, a lovely, attractive lady sat before me in one of my clinics. Her eyes looked sad and weary, and I could see that she was troubled. While giving me an insight into her problems, she had to pause as tears welled up in her eyes. I tried to pacify her, as she was having great difficulty in establishing a coherent conversation with me. When I asked her what age she was, I was surprised when she told me she was 51 years old, as she didn't look any more than 40. I soon found out that she was menopausal, which was confirmed when a hormonal imbalance showed up in her eyes.

When she finally calmed down, she was able to tell me what was troubling her. With hormonal changes, the nervous system can often be affected, and at such times emotions can really get the better of you. This particular lady was absolutely laden with guilt as she had had an extramarital relationship in the early days of her marriage. During the menopause, the guilt she had been harbouring all those years came to the fore, and I had a good talk to her about the life that lay ahead of her. She was now very happily married to the same man on whom she had cheated, but this particular problem was getting in the way of her enjoying life to the full, and she had contemplated talking to her husband about it many times. They were both very happy in their marriage, they had a good life and were proud of their children. The question that arose was should she disturb that relationship or, as she was a Christian, repent for that particular deed and leave it with God? She asked me for advice about what she should do, and I told her the following story, which I have mentioned to several patients before, and advised her in a similar way.

Some years ago, a well-known lawyer came to see me. He had a large office and was well respected in his field. He too was unhappy and was tormented by the thought of something he had done in the past when trying to develop his business. He had a wealthy elderly client. As she had no one to whom she wanted to leave her money, she decided to bequeath her entire estate to a cancer charity. At that time, this man was struggling to get his business established, so when she died he decided to retain some of her money to help set up his own business. Although the amount was not huge, he knew that it was a very selfish deed and that he was effectively stealing. He tried to justify this action by recalling the amount of time he had devoted to this elderly lady, offering her support while she was going through the emotional trauma of facing death. He felt he deserved an extra reward for that.

Some time after the lady died, however, his actions started to plague him. He felt extreme guilt over the matter and was deeply conscious of his wrongdoings. He asked if there was any way I could help him overcome this mentally and physically, and wondered what he could also do to help himself. He in turn was greatly aided by another story I had once heard and which had impressed me. A schoolmistress who was discussing the matter of guilt with her pupils took a large sheet of blank paper and marked a small point in the middle of it with her pencil. She then held it up to the class and asked the children what they could see on this large piece of paper. Of course, they all replied, 'A little black point right in the middle.' She explained to the children that there is forgiveness for every wrongdoing, and when they received forgiveness, then the little black point could be wiped out. I then said to this lawyer, 'I think the best thing you can do with the money you stole is to donate it to cancer research – the same organisation to which the elderly lady had left the rest of her money. You should then look again at that black point in your life, wipe it out and, while doing so, think of all the white space on the paper as a symbol of where you have done good in your life by helping so many others and by putting your life in order.'

On the whole, he was a good man. He helped his clients with their problems and put them at their ease, and he was a good father to his children. Yet he went through life with this burden of guilt on his shoulders, and I am convinced that this was the cause of the rheumatoid arthritis that he suffered from. Once he took my advice, however, and in fact gave the charity double the amount of money that he had held back from the old woman's estate, he was finally able to move on.

The lady to whom I told this story also took my advice to talk things over with her husband and I am happy to say that they got through this difficult time and are now enjoying life together again.

Of course one will feel tormented by guilt if one has an honest attitude in life. With such traumatic experiences, *Arnica* is always of great help, and some homoeopathic remedies that deal with the feelings of guilt can also be used to great effect.

It is reassuring to realise that when we recognise guilt, we can then do something about it. It does no good whatsoever to walk around with matters weighing on your conscience making you miserable. When you experience such thoughts, if you stop and think about it, it is much better to get these feelings out of your system than to leave them there.

A lady consulted me not so long ago. She said that she really didn't want to tell me how bad she had been in her life or about the awful things that she had done, but she wanted some help in trying to rid herself of her guilty feelings. She said that the things she had done in life were so appalling that she found it almost impossible to put them into words. It transpired that she had been responsible for sexual harassment, for threatening people and also for suing people for things of which they were innocent. Although she didn't want to talk about these events in depth, she nevertheless wanted to try to put them behind her.

I told her that it was better to get these thoughts out of her mind and then try to rebuild a new life. Without changing her thoughts and her attitude, she would never be able to move forward. She said, 'I am old, decrepit and miserable, and there is no more music in me. Life is only an existence for me, and I really feel like killing myself.' I reminded her that she still had a soul and that I wanted to take care of that. I gave her a piece of poetry to read at home which was of tremendous help to her. It was entitled 'The Touch of the Master's Hand':

> It was battered and scarred and the auctioneer
> thought it was scarcely worth his while
> to waste much time on an old violin,
> but he held it up with a smile.
> 'What am I bidden, good folks?' he cried,
> 'Who'll start the bidding for me?
> 'A guinea, a guinea, then two. Only two!
> 'Two guineas, and who'll make it three?
> 'Three guineas once, three guineas twice,
> 'going for three,' but no . . .
> From the room far back a grey-haired man
> came forward and picked up the bow.
> Then wiping the dust from the old violin
> and tightening its loosened strings,
> he started to play and the music swelled
> like a carolling angel sings.
>
> The music ceased and the auctioneer,
> in a voice that was quiet and low, said,
> 'What am I bid for the old violin?'
> And he held it up with the bow.

'A thousand guineas and who'll make it two?'
'Two thousand, and who'll make it three?'
'Three thousand once, three thousand twice,
'Going, going and gone,' said he.
The people cheered, but some of them cried,
'We don't quite understand
'what changed its worth.' Swift came the reply,
'The touch of the Master's Hand.'

And many a man with a life out of tune
and battered and scarred with sin,
is auctioned cheap to a thoughtless crowd,
much like that old violin.
A mess of pottage, a glass of wine,
a game, and he travels on.
He is going once, he is going twice,
he is going and almost gone.
But the Master comes and the foolish crowd
can never quite understand
the worth of a soul, and the change that is wrought
by the touch of the Master's Hand.

She later came back to see me and told me that she had
recited this poem over and over again and agreed with me
that, although there was no music left in her, she did still have
a soul. I also gave her acupuncture that helped her to deal
with her feelings of guilt. That lady is now old, and when I see
her from time to time, she always mentions how that poem
changed her life and how she then went on to offer help to
many other people.

When we bury our feelings of guilt, they don't go away but instead gnaw away at us inside. In order to lead a fulfilling life, we have to take responsibility for our actions, and if we have done something that has hurt another person, we have to try to work out a way to make amends. Everybody has done something in life that they feel ashamed about, but we have to tackle those negative feelings of guilt, and then we can start each day afresh.

FIVE

Hate

ONE SATURDAY afternoon, following a week of tireless work in Dublin and Belfast, my penultimate patient of the day was a young, pretty woman. As this was her first consultation, I had to take down her full case history. While I was making notes, the information she was passing to me made me glance up at her several times. She was shaking as she recalled events that had happened to her, and she was deep in thought. As the relevant details of her life unfolded, I could see that she been through a lot of turmoil in her life, resulting in her harbouring an immense amount of hate.

She started to tell me about her youth, which had been difficult at many points due to a father who was aggressive and often drunk. She expressed love for her father and mother, but these problems in her early years had clearly caused her a considerable amount of trauma. Then she grew up, and, I suppose because she was pretty, she had several love affairs, which sadly often ended in disaster. Some of the men with whom she had been romantically involved had made her life a misery, some had deceived her and others had physically assaulted her. These repeated betrayals had led her to become very bitter.

When someone is coping with such serious emotional problems, it is quite common for physical problems to develop, as the immune system is weakened. This young woman had experienced occasional periods of happiness in her life, but the majority of her existence had been overshadowed by unhappiness, and as a result she had fallen ill. She initially caught infections and developed a nasty case of endometriosis. She was an intelligent young lady, but while at the peak of her career as a PA, she started drinking heavily and taking drugs. This resulted in a further deterioration in her health and a total personality change.

She deserved a lot better than the hand that she had been dealt, but unfortunately her story just seemed to go from bad to worse. She became more ill, was admitted to hospital and underwent a lot of operations. She said, 'I wish I had a zip there where my stitches are because I have had to be operated on so often.' Sadly, at the young age of 27, she had to have a total hysterectomy. She also continued to have relationship problems and her second marriage, to an extremely difficult man, broke down. He was self-indulgent and behaved so appallingly towards her that she ended up hating him, and by the time she got rid of him, she was a complete nervous wreck. She was then prescribed incorrect drugs, which led to her developing epilepsy.

There were other episodes during her life that also really shocked me. After another unsuccessful relationship, the man that she had been seeing started to stalk her. This continued over a period of three years and the awful acts that he carried out caused a further deterioration in her health. Eventually he was prosecuted and imprisoned, but this terrible situation had convinced her that she needed to face her problems in a more aggressive manner.

After some further investigation, I carried out a Chinese facial diagnosis and it was obvious that she was very tense and full of hate. Deep down, she was a very nice person with a small but good heart, but unfortunately, she was very misunderstood, and this had left her feeling lonely and in a state of complete despair, worrying about what life was going to bring next. In turn, these feelings of isolation led to her becoming hard and starting to exhibit a lot of anger at the way her life had turned out. Indeed, as she was recounting some of the details of her past, she started to shout and swear, and I could see in her face and by the way she was shaking that she was really in a bad state.

My heart went out to her, and I realised that a lot had to be done to assist her. Due to her health problems, she was now an invalid at the young age of 34 and unable to work. I gave her some advice that day and explained to her that she needed a lot of help. As she didn't have much money, I asked her if she would be agreeable to my using her as a case history for one of my studies in return for any treatment she needed. She agreed and as she stood up to leave, she said to me, 'I know now that there must be a God because, at long last, I have found somebody who will listen to me.' She left with uplifted spirits, and I could already see that some of the stress had lifted from her face.

I had to think deeply about this case, because epilepsy is not easy to get under control, but to get her started I gave her some *Confidence Essence*, which was the most suitable remedy to fit her characteristics and the signature of her character. This remedy helps to boost courage, determination and self-esteem. It contains *Centaury, Pine, Honeysuckle, Larch, Buttercup, Mimulus, Tansy, Walnut, Cerato* and *Elm. Centaury* helps to bring assertiveness, strength, personal power and the ability to draw essential boundaries, making it ideal for those who are prone to being bullied. *Pine* helps to build self-esteem and enables someone to be more understanding of his or her own faults. *Honeysuckle* helps to dissolve memories from the past that may be having a negative influence in the present. *Larch* helps to build confidence, perseverance and objectivity, while *Buttercup* helps someone to recognise and value uniqueness. *Mimulus* helps to bring personal courage, strength and understanding. *Tansy* helps you to move forward with inner clarity, direction and obvious motivation. *Walnut* helps to make you feel protected and encourages you to be adaptable. *Cerato* helps you to trust in yourself and remain uninfluenced by the opinions of others, while *Elm* helps you to be more aware of your capabilities and view your problems in perspective. Adults should take 5 drops of this in a little water 3 times daily, while children (2–7 years) can take 3 drops in a little water 3 times a day. This product is not recommended for children under the age of two and if you are pregnant or breast-feeding you should seek professional healthcare advice before taking this product.

When I left the clinic that day, I was so deep in thought about this girl that I wanted to get home quickly to make more in-depth notes and to work out the most suitable programme for her. There are two ways to reach my house, and I took the shortest route, but this involved travelling on a very narrow road. As my mind was miles away, when the sun blinded me I ran into a car coming in the opposite direction. The other driver turned out to be an orthodox doctor who was out with his family. That was my first ever car accident and I shall never forget it.

So, you can see that from the start I was engrossed with this girl's case. I started to get rid of some of her feelings of hate by using a few of Dr Bach's remedies and I also carried out some acupuncture treatment. She reacted very well to the acupuncture and also to *Avena sativa* from Alfred Vogel. As she was a bad sleeper, I taught her the Hara breathing exercises, which I have described earlier, and gave her some other remedies to try to help her epilepsy. *Cerebrum*, an excellent herbal remedy, and *Viscum album* (mistletoe) had a positive influence on her. I saw her on a weekly basis and she gradually improved. When she comes to see me now, she is very happy and content. She always has a smile on her face, and I seldom hear her swear. Her fits, thankfully, have finally stopped, and her shaking has almost disappeared. This work was so worthwhile, and I was delighted to help someone who was in such despair. Now, when I ask her to do something for me, such as helping out with correspondence, she is only too happy to oblige. What little she can do, she does with devotion, and her life has now taken on a totally different meaning and a positive outlook.

Hate is often born out of jealousy, perhaps because the other person has something for which you yearn – it may be because a work colleague gets promoted instead of you, or that some other person may be more gifted, resulting in feelings of inferiority. It is a very destructive emotion and can negatively influence even strong characters and drive people to commit deeds of which they would never before have considered themselves capable. We have to ask ourselves if there is a way for human beings to overcome hate, a way for hate to be replaced by a positive love. For when hate turns to love, we see some wonderful outcomes.

My old partner, Alfred Vogel, often referred to the interesting story in the Old Book about Cain and Abel. Cain believed that God favoured Abel over him and became jealous. Then, filled with anger and hate, he murdered his brother Abel. When God asked him where his brother was, Cain replied, 'Am I my brother's keeper?'

In answer to this, I would say that we are all each other's keepers. We live in a world today where we see so much hate and so little love. There are many different causes, but one of the most pernicious is jealousy over material possessions. We have to get over this, and it is miraculous to see that when people with these feelings adopt a spirit of love and try to do their best, how successful they can become. We have to learn to share what we have with each other. We need to consider what we can do to help the people of this world understand that it needs peace and love.

I greatly admire one of my cousins whose life is completely devoted to helping others, a characteristic that my mother unquestionably had, and I often reflect on what my cousin says: 'You have to love your neighbour as yourself.' The girl that I spoke about earlier had lost the ability to love herself, so she could not help others. We have to learn to love ourselves, and when we are able to do this and look after ourselves, we can then love our neighbour, which is very important. If we get our priorities right, we can do a lot to help this poor world. When there are feelings of hate, work positively to eliminate them. Use flower remedies – there are several suitable ones and, especially when one makes a wrong decision, *Emergency Essence* is a wonderful remedy. Use some natural remedies, such as *Avena sativa* or *Zincum valerianicum*, to help overcome negative feelings and then try hard to replace these with positive ones. You should then be comforted by the fact that you have managed to overcome your feelings of hate, and by doing so you will have enriched your life.

SIX

Jealousy

JEALOUSY IS a very powerful and often dangerous emotion that can be linked with all kinds of other negative feelings, like anxiety, fear, hate and loneliness. Commonly termed 'the green-eyed monster', this is a well-deserved label, because it really is a monster – and one that can do untold harm.

We all understand its negativity, and most of us try to keep this emotion under wraps. Feelings of jealousy, although extremely common, are not something many of us care to admit to. This is why I often have to dig very deeply into the recesses of a patient's psyche to reach the conclusion that their malady is rooted in jealousy.

There is, of course, a big difference between jealousy and envy. Envy is a much milder emotion and, again, is one we all feel from time to time. It is only natural to feel envious of, perhaps, a lovely new house, or the story of a wonderful holiday. But such feelings can be quickly rationalised and put into perspective. The old-fashioned saying 'count your blessings' is often a very pertinent one. We should all try to remember the things in life that we can be thankful for. And we should also remember that we never know what lives people really lead behind the closed doors of that idyllic house, or within the confines of that luxurious cabin on a cruise liner. The grass isn't always greener.

Sadly, however, it is increasingly common in today's materialistic world for people to feel jealous – of their partners, their friends, their colleagues at work or their neighbours. I was once the target of four medical doctors who tried to discredit my work, and it was a very unpleasant experience. So jealousy can affect not only the person experiencing it but also the target.

In this age of so-called celebrity, we see a multitude of magazines aimed at women, featuring photographs of beautiful models. These models are the very image of perfection, but who made them that way? In many cases it was not Mother Nature but the skill of the person who carried out the digital manipulation or airbrushing, to give it its common name. The photographs are actually a form of cheating, and I have heard it said that even the models themselves wished they really looked like that!

But try telling that to the young, impressionable girl who sees only an impossibly high standard of beauty – the peachy, blemish-free skin, sparkling eyes, silky thick hair and endless legs – a standard that she cannot meet. And so the seeds of discontent are sown. The jealousy that arises with the teenager wanting to look like the models she sees in magazines and hating what she sees when she looks in the mirror can result in a lifetime of misery. It can invade all areas of the victim's life – her work, her friendships, her relationships and so on. Unless dealt with, it can lead to many serious problems. For example, it can lead to alcohol or drug abuse and even mental illness. Eating disorders and poor body image affect millions of people in the world.

I cringe when I hear the use of the word 'ugly' when applied to a fellow human being. There are ugly buildings and ugly thoughts, but no work of Mother Nature – whether animal, plant or human – is truly ugly. No one is perfect, but we all have unique qualities – both mental and physical – which, together, create a special and beautiful mind, body and soul.

In any case, what is generally perceived as the gift of beauty does not automatically lead to happiness. I can tell you that those we consider to be beautiful are often very unhappy and dissatisfied with both their physical appearance and their lives in general. This may be mystifying, but it is true.

A top model who consulted me told of a life devoid of true friendship. As a teenager, she found her offers of friendship rejected. The boys she liked turned her down. She was lonely and formed the opinion that something was wrong with her. This led to her becoming very shy, and she became very aloof and removed from her peers. In turn, they thought she was conceited and shunned her. I handed her a small mirror and asked her to look in it and tell me what she saw. I know what I saw – a beautiful face but with sad eyes that lacked sparkle and vitality. 'I just see my face,' she said.

'Do you think it is beautiful?' I enquired.

'No,' she replied.

I knew she was giving what she felt was a genuine answer, and it pained me.

There was a lot of help I could offer this woman to build her confidence, and eventually I saw her eyes sparkle, and I'm delighted to say she went on to have a successful career and marriage. But her feelings of inadequacy, which stemmed from the jealousy directed at her as a teenager, will remain deep inside her, and she will have to remain strong in certain situations to stop them from resurfacing. A lot depends on a person's support network of friends and family. A strong, encouraging network goes far to keep people stable and happy.

I have talked about a victim of jealousy, now I come to those who are experiencing jealousy towards other individuals of their acquaintance. This is also difficult to deal with, especially when, as already mentioned, it is hard to get people to admit to such feelings. Jealousy is still a taboo subject and people often try to bury it rather than acknowledge it even to themselves, never mind to other people.

As a holistic practitioner concerned with mind, body and soul, I do believe that there can be an emotional input to almost every disease or physical complaint. Often, I intuitively sense the root of the problem after just a few simple questions. At other times, I need to probe carefully to try to ascertain what is behind the mask.

A young woman came to me complaining of terrible headaches. I discovered she only suffered them while at work in a large open-plan office. They didn't affect her away from this environment, which led to the simple conclusion that they were work related. We had to consider the physical surroundings. Was it the air conditioning or chemicals that were being used in the office? Or was it the pressure of the job or a domineering supervisor? Was she capable of doing the job? Did she have low blood sugar? Was she drinking too much caffeine? Was she dehydrated?

Initially, I didn't think there could be any jealousy involved because she was such a self-confident, attractive person with every physical attribute she could wish for. But having exhausted almost every possibility, I was about to give up when she revealed her dislike for one particular colleague. It turned out she despised – and I use the word with care – another young woman who was very pretty and to whom all the men in the office were attracted.

In fact, my patient hated this woman so much that she admitted sending her anonymous evil notes and stealing things from her desk. As she told me this, tears were streaming down her face. I admit I was taken aback, because to my eyes she had no need to be jealous. Here before me was a beautiful woman, so why was she experiencing such strong emotions, which were manifesting themselves in debilitating headaches?

She told me that her first boyfriend had undermined her self-esteem by criticising aspects of her appearance. He told her she had short legs and an oversized bottom, and he refused to make love to her unless she was wearing suspenders, stockings and stiletto heels. I could see the pain in her face as she confessed this, and I knew then that this boyfriend had been jealous of this lovely young woman – another incidence of the destructiveness of this horrid emotion. It wasn't just a fetish he had for certain items of underwear; he made demeaning remarks about her body and deliberately upset her.

I wondered why she had stayed with such a man. She said she complied with his wishes because she adored him at the time. She added that she eventually left him when he started physically abusing her as well as making unreasonable demands.

She was left with deep scars that took quite a while to heal. I was able to help her with acupuncture and various treatments and remedies, and I also referred her for a specialist course on energy balancing.

I am glad to say that this story has a happy ending. The woman actually made friends with the object of her earlier jealousy, and they became close allies in the office and a great support to each other.

It is often the case that these deep-rooted feelings of inadequacy stem from childhood, when misguided parents give the wrong messages to their children.

All little girls are pretty and all little boys are handsome, and usually no more so than in the eyes of their devoted parents. But alas, sometimes a parent can say things to a child – knowingly or unknowingly – that leave a lasting imprint on that child's mind. One patient told me that her father said she looked like a monkey and would never find a boyfriend. Maybe he was joking, but to that little girl it was no joke, and the thought of this blighted her life and impeded her progress in all areas. Every time she looked in the mirror, she saw the face of a monkey.

Why her father chose to make such a remark is unfathomable. It is, however, quite possible that he had deep psychological problems of his own. Those who have what psychologists describe as 'character disorders' tend to make disastrous parents. They are capable of saying the most hurtful things to their children while remaining blissfully unaware of having done so. It is possible that such parents are jealous of their children, and, of course, there are occasions when children are jealous of their parents.

Now I will discuss an area in which almost all of us have felt a bit of jealousy – within the realm of sexual relationships. Who hasn't felt a little twinge of green on observing their partner giving undivided attention to a member of the opposite sex? This is perfectly normal and can even be considered positive. It can make the partner aware of the desirability of their mate and encourage them to work hard at making sure they remain attractive to him or her. In other words, it discourages complacency in a relationship and can even ignite the flame of desirability.

One woman I know has a husband who is regularly given attention by lots of women because of the nature of his work. His wife likes this and finds it keeps their romance alive. She obviously has a good sense of self-worth and is secure in his love. She doesn't feel she is going to lose him to one of his admirers. If she had suffered from low self-esteem, she might have felt extremely threatened by his admirers, and this could have been a destructive force in their relationship.

As gregarious human beings, we all like being admired and given attention, but what is harmless flirtation to one person can be seen as dangerous behaviour by another. Some people – often those who work in the public eye – require to have their egos rubbed with regularity, and if this is seen by a jealous spouse, it can cause no end of trouble. Perhaps this is why celebrity relationships are notoriously rocky.

Sadly, I encounter a fair number of women who have been married to jealous husbands for so long that they are literally wasting away. This type of husband makes sure his wife is kept down. He doesn't encourage her to have her own friendships or social life, and her life has to revolve around him and any children they might have. He is controlling and sometimes violent. If there is no violence in the relationship, the control can be veiled so that the wife is not aware of it. Such men can be very clever and are real experts at their craft, so that if the wife feels she has a problem, she rarely suspects the husband. Often it is obvious to outsiders what is going on.

One common technique used by such men is to give their wives affectionate but uncomplimentary pet names such as 'podgy', 'piggy wiggy' or 'thunder thighs'. He will use this name while embracing his wife and smiling happily so she has no idea that it is actually a controlling put-down.

One woman told me that she had to do something about her awful cellulite before her husband left her for another woman. I asked her to show me it. She had none, not a tiny bit. In fact, she was blessed with flawless skin. She insisted she had cellulite because her husband had told her she had.

As I thought about this later, I wondered if her husband

was jealous of his wife because she had such a good figure and general appearance. Maybe he wanted to create fictional imperfections that would play on her mind and make her feel unattractive to other men and grateful to her husband for tolerating her. This could stem from the husband's low self-esteem and feelings of inadequacy. It is likely he was jealous of his wife's vibrancy and felt sure he would lose her to a better man. In such cases, I feel sad for both parties, and they require a lot of help and counselling to overcome these difficulties.

Of course, it is not only men who can make their partners' lives a misery. Women can wreak havoc in relationships in the name of jealousy, too. Some women live in fear that their husbands will stray, so they try to control their men and make sure they don't have any opportunities to meet other women. Obviously, this is another recipe for disaster. It can even result in the person who is being controlled actually doing what the partner is trying to prevent because he feels so smothered and unhappy.

If you have a jealous partner, you have a difficult life. It is as simple as that. They will endeavour to make your life difficult, and if they are not careful, they will make themselves repulsive in your eyes, spelling the end of the relationship. In my opinion, more relationships are destroyed by jealousy than anything else. Those who are secure and love themselves tend to be less jealous of others and less possessive of partners.

The foundation for jealousy is insecurity. A jealous person may believe that their partner is keeping something hidden from them. This may or may not be true. The jealous person has thoughts like 'she is bound to meet someone else at work' or 'she will leave me because I am so unattractive'. They need reassurance and lots of it. They need to communicate their feelings, to be open and honest. If it all stays hidden, the relationship will deteriorate.

Again, the root cause of the jealousy can often be found in a person's childhood. If a child sees either parent being unfaithful, he or she can find it difficult to accept that his or her partner will not do likewise. A male patient told me that he regularly saw his stepmother disappearing with the ice-cream man while his dad was on night shift. This led to him having suspicions about his own wife, even though she gave him no reason.

Some research says that jealousy is an 'adaptive evolutionary mechanism'. In other words, men are jealous because they want to make sure that it is *their* genes that are carried on, while women are jealous because they want to ensure protection, shelter and food for their young.

There could be some truth in this theory, but wherever jealousy comes from there is no doubt that it is rife in today's society, and it is causing far too much heartache and physical illness.

Jealousy really is a monster, and in its extreme forms it can lead to terrible crimes like murder. When it appears in your life as a mere flicker, acknowledge it and deal with it. Don't allow it to really catch alight and smoulder away until irrevocable damage is caused.

We live in a material world where some have so much and others have so little in terms of wealth and possessions. On a global scale, it seems to me that peace will be hard to attain when there are such extremes of poverty and wealth.

Those who, either through hard work, sheer talent or a helping hand from families, have the trappings of success – the properties, cars, jewellery, designer clothes – are often victims of jealousy. But looking at many of the wealthiest families in history, it is patently obvious that money does not always bring happiness. It can buy many things, but it doesn't buy contentment. That stems from strong feelings of self-esteem and the knowledge that you love and are loved.

So how, generally, do I deal with cases of jealousy? Well, as I have said, jealousy is often the root cause of a problem, and by the time the person reaches the point of asking me for help, the emotional aspect has a physical manifestation which is shouting out to be dealt with. There are many treatment possibilities, including physical therapies and herbal remedies such as *Zincum valerianicum*. Acupuncture is excellent at allowing energies to flow freely, thus releasing negativity and blockages – osteopathy is also effective in this regard. My flower essences work at a vibrational level that can be releasing and empowering, and homoeopathy can also be very useful. Massage can be wonderful at assisting people to reconnect with their bodies and begin to love themselves, especially when assisted by the use of potent essential oils. Healing energy therapies (like reiki) can be a catalyst for change in cases of buried emotions. And there are many more.

There is a lot that can be done, but the biggest leap of all is when the person acknowledges the jealousy, in whatever form, that is behind the superficial malady. This is in itself a powerful purge of the poison. Once this watershed point is reached, there is no going back – the improvement in the patient's physical condition is almost guaranteed, as is the joy which comes from a freeing of the spirit. It truly is emotional healing.

Feeling jealous is human and natural. It is nothing to be ashamed of. What matters is how we deal with such feelings, and this depends largely on how strong our inner support system is. The quicker the situation is dealt with the better. Bring it out and clear it out. Don't allow jealous emotions to fester and don't bury them. One day you will be forced to deal with them. Don't lose a good friend because of jealousy. Time after time I hear of friendships where one person just switches off and cuts out the other with no explanation. It can often be surmised that jealousy is the reason.

One woman told me, in tears, that her best friend had severed all contact between them. This was extremely hurtful, and all her attempts to contact the friend were rebuffed. She will never be sure, but she reached the conclusion that her newly announced pregnancy, which came not long after her friend's miscarriage, was the reason.

Baby or child jealousy can be a heartbreaking problem. Children are often a measure of success in today's society. Those who find they are infertile, for whatever reason, are open to a myriad of uneasy emotions.

There can even be jealousy over the number of children in a family. A woman told me she hated her husband because he had only allowed her to have two children. She knew this was sensible and was grateful to have one of each sex. Then, when she accidentally became pregnant, he persuaded her to have a termination. Years later, she started feeling jealous of anyone who had more than two children. She reasoned that she was lucky to have a healthy boy and girl, but still the feelings wouldn't go away. She found herself looking at fathers of more than two children and concluding that they must love their wives more than her husband loved her. Her feelings were irrational, but they were also deep seated and could not be ignored. I knew that this was a serious problem, and that her relationship with her husband was in dire straits. The crux of the matter was that he had 'forced' her to have the termination. She required lengthy counselling, and after this she decided to leave her husband to search for new happiness – which she found in the company of cats on a remote island.

This kind of problem often lies dormant until the children have grown up, as in this case, and the mother has time on her hands to reflect.

Another difficult time for women – and to a lesser extent men, too – is the stage leading up to and around the menopause. Women can feel they are losing their attractiveness and feel jealous of younger women, and men can have the same feelings towards younger, fitter men. This, again, is quite normal and in most cases can be easily overcome with a little mental adjustment and perhaps the assistance of a flower essence. Sometimes it is the right time to look for a new direction in life, new interests and new people.

When we go through experiences in life, we come to learn who our true friends really are. As I mentioned earlier, there was one point in my life when I was disappointed about the feelings of jealousy and greed that were being directed towards me, and I found myself in the middle of a conspiracy. In the midst of all that, I received this piece of poetry written by Roy Croft. I studied that particular piece of poetry many times and it became very dear to me during that difficult period in my life because I then realised what a real friend means, after all.

> *I love you,*
> *not only for what you are*
> *but for what I am*
> *when I am with you.*
> *I love you,*
> *not only for what*
> *you have made of yourself*
> *but for what*
> *you are making of me.*
> *I love you*
> *for the part of me*
> *that you bring out.*
> *I love you*
> *for putting your hand*
> *into my heaped-up heart*
> *and passing over*
> *all the foolish, weak things*
> *that you can't help*
> *dimly seeing there,*
> *and for the drawing out*
> *into the light*
> *all the beautiful belongings*
> *that no one else had looked*
> *quite far enough to find.*
> *I love you because you*
> *are helping me to make*
> *of the lumber of my life*

not a tavern
but a temple;
out of works
of my every day
not a reproach
but a song.
I love you
because you have done
more than any creed
could have done
to make me good,
and more than any fate
could have done
to make me happy.
You have done it
without a touch,
without a word,
without a sign.
You have done it
by being yourself.
Perhaps that is what
being a friend means,
after all.

I wish to end this chapter on an optimistic note. One of the founders of the Findhorn Foundation, a spiritual community in the north of Scotland, Eileen Caddy, who died in December 2006, had to deal with her own difficult emotions when her husband left her for another woman. This remarkable woman managed to find the peace that lives deep in all of us. In relation to her husband leaving her for a younger woman, she said,

'Could I love someone enough to see him leave me for someone else, and hold no bitterness, resentment or jealousy? Of course I couldn't. At least not without God's help.' I conclude that to be jealous is to be human. So, if you need help, reach out, whether to God or to your fellow man, and you will receive it.

SEVEN

Depression

LEVELS OF emotional stress and depression are at the highest they have ever been, and it is estimated that annual prescriptions for antidepressants in England have soared to over 22 million. It is estimated that at any one time between 10 per cent and 20 per cent of the population will be experiencing depressive symptoms, with roughly twice as many women as men being affected. General symptoms include lowness of mood, lack of interest and enjoyment in usual activities, decreased energy levels, tiredness, sleep disturbance, poor concentration and altered appetite, but there are various kinds of depression, and it is for psychiatrists to define the kind of depression they are treating in order to determine the best approach.

I believe that more medical research still needs to be carried out to help those with depression overcome the problems facing them today. Some prescribed drugs may initially appear to alleviate certain symptoms of depression, but they can also have dangerous side effects. If there is a way to treat depression naturally, then make this your first choice. You will then have the advantage of overcoming this problem without experiencing the dreadful side effects you can get from prescribed drugs.

Depression can strike anyone unexpectedly. Patients suffering from depression are often bewildered and wonder what is happening to them, and it can be very worrying and upsetting for those around them, too. This was precisely the case with a family who consulted me recently. The wife of the gentleman in question was extremely worried about her husband's behaviour and wondered how to explain this to their children.

I studied this patient, who sat without any glimmer of hope in his face, looking into a dark future that lay before him. My heart went out to him. His wife told me that he had generally been a happy man until, out of the blue, he became slightly depressed. A long list of drugs was prescribed over time, and even two chemists queried who had prescribed these strong drugs. Rather than being helped by this medication, the man became more and more withdrawn and even felt suicidal. His family wondered what could be done to help him.

His wife told me that he was a good Christian who knew the Bible off by heart, but he had lost all faith and hope for the future. I started to talk to him by asking if he had grandchildren, and he said that he had. I then asked how much time he spent with them, but, because of his depression, he showed no interest in them at all. I gleaned from the short responses he gave that he felt he had nothing to look forward to and that in his mind his future looked bleak. Yet he was young enough to do some wonderful work.

As a way of demonstrating that people cared greatly about him, I mentioned how comforting it must be to him that his children were so concerned that they had accompanied him to see me and that his grandchildren also wanted to help him. I then mentioned to him that at one period in my own life when I became deeply depressed about something that had happened, my eldest granddaughter had been of tremendous help to me. She coaxed me to go to Croatia with her for a few days, as she knew that I had wanted to see a professor of herbalism there. That visit turned out to be a lesson for me, because I too had lost some faith in life. At that point, he started to look up and take an interest in what I was saying.

I explained that when I arrived in Croatia, feeling quite down and depressed, we had to make a two-and-a-half hour trip to our final destination. At a certain point on our journey, the driver told us that we had reached one of the highest sites in Croatia. I looked around, and I was so impressed with what I saw that I begged him to stop, but he told me he couldn't. He wasn't allowed. I wanted to spend some time there to take in more of the beautiful panorama that surrounded us, and in that moment I suddenly realised that this is one of the most common mistakes we all make. We are all in such a rush in our journey of life that we often do not take the time to stop and look around, and in that way we can miss out on the best that life has to offer.

I told my patient that although he was in a deep valley at the moment, he had to come out of it again, and his faith would help him on his difficult journey. I added that this experience of mine was a reminder to us all of the great possibilities that we come across in life to help us regain our faith. We can all make these possibilities a reality, and even though we can sometimes be disappointed in even our best friends, we still have this invisible friend who is always with us. He is always there, but we have to regain our faith.

This reminds me of the little girl whose father told her that Christ would always be by her side. Wherever this little girl went, she would always make sure there was a space next to her, and when her father asked why she did this, she said, 'I have to leave a space so that Christ can be with me.'

I told this patient, who was clearly suffering, that that friend was still there for him, although he needed to believe again, and he had to make the effort to climb out of the deep valley of depression and then climb as high as he could so that he could see things clearly once more.

When Christ took three of his disciples up a steep mountain, they had a deep conversation. It was a difficult mountain to climb, and the three disciples were delighted when they reached the summit, as they loved it as much as I loved that high point in Croatia. When they reached the summit, they saw Jesus become radiant and speak with Moses and Elijah, and God called him His son. The three disciples might have been exhausted after their long climb, but they had one focus in their lives and that was to see Christ. When they opened their eyes, that was all they saw when they looked up. But I have always wondered how the other disciples felt. The three who went up saw this wonderful vision. They saw Christ as their Saviour, but the other nine were perhaps too busy to accompany them and could only wonder about what had happened. But one thing we all know is that Christ promised to be with us always – it is a promise to everyone, and, as I told this patient, it was a promise to him also. Problems might seem like mountains, but we won't overcome them if we sit at the base of the mountain. We have to climb up, and I told this man that this was what he had to do.

What a change my chat made to that man's life. It was quite astonishing that this story had such an impact on him. Following our meeting he started to pick up the pieces of his life, and as his depression slowly lifted he gradually reduced his prescribed antidepressants. I gave him some help in the form of acupuncture, remedies and also some relaxation exercises. Each time I saw him, he had improved a bit more, because he had started to focus on the future again. He mustered up enough enthusiasm to make his life a lot better than it had ever been previously.

Interestingly, when thinking of this man's strong faith, one of the remedies I gave him had a holy name – *Holy Basil Trinity Blend*. Holy basil or *Ocimum sanctum* has been grown in India for over 3,000 years and is still highly valued today. Known also as Tulsi, it is an important symbol in the Hindu religion and is believed to encourage positivity and increased awareness. In a scientific study, a herbal preparation that combines holy basil along with three other Ayurvedic herbs was shown to improve the body's ability to adapt to stress. It seems to work by supporting the immune system and building the body's immunity to disease.

As time progressed, I gave him *Mood Essence*, a flower essence which is a brilliant combination of several flowers, together with *Avena sativa*. As he had a troublesome stomach problem, he also took *Centaurium*.

Centaurium acts as a bitter tonic and digestive stimulant and owes its action to a group of compounds called bitter glycosides. The taste of these substances stimulates the appetite and triggers the secretion of digestive juices in the stomach, improving the breakdown of food. At the same time, the hormone gastrin is secreted from the walls of the stomach. This enhances gastric motility and relaxes the pyloric sphincter, which allows food to pass out of the stomach more easily. The tone of the oesophageal sphincter is also increased, preventing reflux of food from the stomach back into the oesophagus, a process that is responsible for the symptoms of heartburn.

The recommended dose for adults is 15 drops, 3 times a day in a little water. Children should take 1 drop per year of age (2–10 years) in a little water. An adjustment to the recommended dosages may be required due to individual differences in the sensitivity to bitter herbs. Ideally, *Centaurium*, like all bitter herbs, should be taken fifteen minutes before meals. It should always be taken in a little water, sipped and held in the mouth before swallowing, to stimulate its action. This product is not recommended for pregnant or nursing women unless directed by a healthcare professional. There are no restrictions on long-term use.

This patient has made very good progress, and I am so pleased that he is once again able to cope with the journey of life.

It is easy to become depressed and miserable, but we have to do everything we can to lift ourselves out of it. When I was in Canada, a young girl came to see me. She had been diagnosed with ME and was justifiably depressed. It took me a long time to connect with her, though I got the impression that she wanted to open up to me. After some time, I asked her to be honest with me and tell me the truth about what had happened to her. It was then that I discovered she had been raped. This resulted in a serious depression, and as she felt too ashamed and embarrassed to talk to her parents about it she went into a deep decline and became isolated. This unfortunate girl became so ill that she needed urgent help, which thankfully I was able to give her.

I gave her some homoeopathic remedies that can make a huge difference, such as *Staphysagria*, and I could see an almost instant improvement. After that, I had to rebuild her health and used *Quick Immune Response* from Michael's, which is an excellent remedy for the immune system, and a series of flower essences, such as *Confidence Essence*, *Vitality Essence* and *Emergency Essence*, which all helped her a great deal. After some time, she luckily returned to her normal self.

Hypericum perforatum (St John's Wort) also had a great part to play in her recovery. It is a very interesting remedy and is particularly helpful in treating mild to moderate depression, Seasonal Affective Disorder (SAD) and viral infections.

We now know that this herb has specific actions that influence the chemical neurotransmitters in the brain, and in recent studies it has been found to be beneficial in alleviating many symptoms associated with depression when taken over a four-week period, without the side effects experienced with conventional antidepressant medication. For example, it does not cause drowsiness, so it can be used when driving or operating machinery. It is available as tincture, fresh herb tablets and as an oil. When applied externally as an oil, it is a valuable antibacterial, anti-inflammatory remedy that will aid in the healing of burns, wounds and infections.

New evidence does suggest that *Hypericum* preparations may interfere with certain other medication, so patients on prescribed medication should consult their doctors before using it. Patients currently taking *Hypericum*, who are subsequently prescribed medication or buy medication from a pharmacy, must tell their doctor or pharmacist that they are taking this remedy. Exposure to the sun while taking *Hypericum* may result in a skin reaction. This is more common when it is applied externally.

St John's Wort is often portrayed as the natural Prozac. Indeed a lot of people have slowly weaned themselves off Prozac and used *St John's Wort* as an effective natural alternative.

This was the case with a middle-aged lady who consulted me. During the menopause, she became a Jekyll and Hyde character, but her symptoms were alleviated when I prescribed *St John's Wort*, and she told me she was so relieved that she could laugh again.

Laughter is a great medicine in lifting depression. My grandfather also said that singing was a great help, even if you did not feel like it. It is worthwhile remembering that it only takes 14 muscles to smile but 72 to frown.

Some people, however, can be so deep in depression that they can't find anything to smile about. One busy morning, I got on to a packed Tube train at Marylebone Street to go to my Hadley Wood clinic, with my last stop being Cockfosters. In front of where I stood were a young mother and her small child. The child was eating some brightly coloured sweets and the mother a large packet of crisps. Once in a while, the mother moaned, and when the carriage became less crowded, I sat next to her. Nowadays, it is not normal to talk to anyone while travelling on the Underground, so I was surprised when this lady started to grumble and tell me how bad she felt. I enquired why she specifically chose me to tell. 'Well,' she said, 'you are the television doctor, so perhaps you can help me.'

When I listened to her story of how depressed she was, of how her husband beat her up and about her unhealthy diet, my heart went out to her. As we talked, she asked if she could continue on the journey with me until I reached my destination, as she wanted to talk further to me. After listening to all that she had to say, I recommended some remedies to her that would help to alleviate her symptoms, and as she did not have a lot of money I sent these to her. Although I never saw her again, she has kept in touch with me since that first meeting, and I am so glad that I was able to help her recover from her difficult situation. She now leads a normal life, feeling much healthier after having lost six stones overall. At the time that I met her, she was suicidal, and I think if it hadn't been for her child she would have ended her life long ago, not knowing then that it would only have taken some small adjustments to help her.

It often needs no more than a small change to improve a situation. Have we forgotten the art of talking to one another? Do we not take the time to listen to people who are depressed, or are they in so much turmoil that they don't want to talk about their problems? Research has discovered that it has become much less common for people to turn to a minister, priest or religious leader for guidance these days, and although religion can give people a sense of belonging and a friendship with Christ, sometimes people lose sight of the light at the end of the tunnel. In saying that, it is important to remember that the sun can shine again even for those who have lost sight of any ray of hope.

So many people are hurt by the injustice and misunderstanding in today's society that I often wonder what humanity is coming to. A man comes to my mind of whom I am fond, and I also know his family. He is unfortunately in religious turmoil and became a manic depressive, often acting like a zombie. He suffered with problems like anorexia nervosa and bulimia, and said he sometimes felt so depressed that he had an overwhelming pain. It is often difficult to accurately diagnose depression. When I see him sometimes and talk to him, I feel so sorry for him. I have tried to help him, but he is so fixed in his own ideas that neither a psychiatrist nor a therapist can help him at this moment.

On another occasion, I was consulted by a depressed man who had lost his wife. He was very angry, displaying the usual symptoms of grief, but he then started to become violent. Luckily I was able to help him and he eventually picked up the pieces of his life. I got him interested in the hospice where they had been so kind to him when his wife was dying. Because of their compassion, he wanted to aid their finances by raising as much money as he could for them, and he now has a full-time job there. He tells me that he was able to overcome his negative depression and instead adopt a positive attitude to life, and he now makes use of that positivity by doing all he can to help the people who are so poorly there.

When depression can be overcome and the sufferer can take positive action in life, this can lead to a wonderful feeling of fulfilment. When this particular man told me he felt worthless when he first came to see me, I told him what I have told so many patients before – that even if they feel they are just a drop in the ocean, they are still part of that great ocean, and there is always so much work that they can do to benefit others.

Sometimes seemingly insurmountable problems can have a relatively simple solution. An attractive lady came to me the other day, feeling very down following the birth of her best friend's baby. For about 12 years, she and her husband had tried for a baby but they had been unsuccessful. She told me that she had really started to hate this friend. Fortunately, I was able to alter that view by giving her some *Heather*, a flower essence from Dr Bach, together with my own essence, *Mood Essence*, and finally an essence specially formulated to suit her problems. What a transformation there was! I then suggested that we should try to find out why she had not been able to conceive. I carried out some tests, and everything was fine with both her husband and herself, although both were quite depressed. It wasn't until she told me that she had problems with her back that I wondered if this could be the cause. I had a good look at it and could find very little wrong, but I suggested that she should have a scan, which she did. Following that, she saw a gynaecologist, who discovered that a piece of bone was actually blocking eggs that she was producing during ovulation. To cut a long story short, within three months of an operation to remove that piece of bone, she became pregnant. A totally different picture then emerged, with a much happier lady who had overcome a problem that could have been detrimental to her long-term health.

During pregnancy, she needed some extra help, and following a course of acupuncture and the prescription of some homoeopathic remedies including *Nux vomica,* she produced a healthy baby. This changed her whole life, and both she and her husband were happy again.

I remember clearly a nice gentleman who came to work for me in the late 1950s in the first clinic I had in Holland. He told me that he was a great believer in the benefits of colour, song and music, so I asked him why. He said, 'Well, I was very depressed and had a very negative outlook on life. Being a music teacher, I felt that I should be able to lift myself out of it if I could just hit the right note with my listeners.' He felt that there was not enough emotion in his music to satisfy his listeners, so he worked hard at changing this. Although he was a skilled musician, he felt that his music lacked passion. He was desperate to get it right, but he couldn't seem to find the right pitch, as he called it, even with his musical talents. He said that although mechanically the frequencies were all precise, he had to discover how to adjust his music so that the listener would be moved by it. Following much hard work, he saw by people's reactions that there was a sound in his music that they enjoyed. He said that music had to be played to the whole body and not just to the ears, and the individual frequencies had to touch people. That was why he had felt that his music was lacking something and would not be right until he achieved this goal. He felt that the whole body should be on a wavelength with the one who played the music. The pitch had to be set so that it would be tuned in to the ear of the listener. Isn't this the case in life? Harmony is important in everything. Harmony between mind, body and soul is more vital than anything else.

This brings me to the story of a young man who gave me his life history and then said that he felt he had come to the end of his life – he couldn't fight any more. He said that after much prompting, praying and trying to get his life into order and harmony, he totally broke down and was taken to hospital. He was released after getting some treatment but then found himself completely alone again. There was nobody who could help him. For days, he walked the streets and tried to find help. For days, he cried. When he finally went back home, he felt there was no help out there for him. The final blow came when he lost his job, and he completely lost faith in everything. He said that in this time of great need, he had phoned our helpline and finally found someone who was willing to listen to him and sympathise with his situation. His biggest problem was constant diarrhoea, and in order to stop this he was advised to take *Tormentil Complex* from Alfred Vogel. The other remedy he was prescribed was *Ginkgo biloba,* which can give a patient a very good lift and help improve circulation, which can be sluggish in someone suffering from depression. Following his recovery, he wrote a letter of thanks to me saying: 'One, I wake up fresh in the morning; two, I have learned to forgive; three, I can smile and laugh again; four, I lost my excess weight; five, I continue to make a positive difference to my life; and, six, I am able to control and banish all forms of negative thinking. This was my toughest battle of all but I am now back to normal.' Such letters always give me great hope that we can enjoy a worthwhile life again even when we think it has ebbed away.

One extremely busy day when I was practising in Edinburgh, a fairly young woman, particularly emotional and depressed, came into my clinic. I spoke to her briefly and recommended that she would obtain benefit from taking a few remedies, but most importantly I suggested that she should try some acupuncture. After two or three treatments, I found such an immense improvement that I asked my colleague, Charmaine Shepherd, who is of Dutch origin, to give me her thoughts on the treatment that she gives for emotional problems using various forms of acupuncture while complementing this with some other methods and herbal medicine. She wrote down some interesting information for me, and I asked her permission to include it in this book.

She wrote about the subject of the emotions, mind and spirit and traditional Chinese medicine (TCM), where the spirit is gaining more attention as science begins to unravel the mystery of the connections between the brain, endocrine, immune and nervous systems. Although the links are not yet fully understood, there is convincing evidence that emotions have a powerful effect on health and vice versa. Chinese medicine has for more than 5,000 years studied emotions as the cause of disease and has documented ideas about how emotions can lead to physical symptoms. TCM practitioners therefore acknowledge underlying emotional causes in disease and will treat the person accordingly.

Thoughts and emotions can influence the glands, the immune system, the autonomic nervous system, the skin, muscles, intestines, heart, circulation and breathing. The physical symptoms that result from emotional causes are the body's way of communicating to us that we need to resolve certain issues. It is therefore important for us to learn to recognise our emotions and listen to their messages, so that we can use them in a positive, constructive and non-damaging way.

Being realistic, we cannot avoid being angry, sad, afraid or aggrieved in the course of our lives. The death of somebody close to us, for example, will naturally provoke grief. However, if these emotions are excessive or prolonged, it would appear that they can then become a cause of disease. On the other hand, many emotions are considered healthy and provide us with the mental energy and determination to go through life. In TCM, it is believed that the way that we manage emotions makes them either harmful or beneficial. Anger, for instance, can be either dissipated in an outburst of fury or it can be harnessed to provide the courage and drive to achieve goals. So, learning to recognise and acknowledge emotions can help us in healing. In TCM, emotions are believed to create an energetic resonance that influences our health. If we can harness the power of our emotions, we are able to bring about physical healing!

Anger affects the liver

This includes resentment, frustration, bitterness, etc. The symptoms usually show in the head and neck – headaches, tinnitus, dizziness and a red face. Often when people are frustrated, they might end up drinking alcohol, which is very toxic to the liver. While the alcohol might give a short-term sensation of relaxation, the liver will suffer more as a result.

Repressed anger can often appear as depression. This usually happens when it is not appropriate to show anger, usually to someone in authority. The person may show all the signs of depression, such as losing interest in life, but they are like a volcano waiting to erupt. In these cases, there are usually liver symptoms accompanying the depression, such as swollen and tender breasts and PMS in women, headaches or hypertension. These symptoms are messages from our organs, and in this case we should nurture the liver with herbs such as *Milk Thistle* while also finding a constructive outlet for the anger, such as sport, and addressing the underlying cause of the anger, for example by learning to be more assertive.

This brings to mind a patient who came into the clinic with severe and chronic pain in the area of the liver. He had started drinking heavily to ease the pain, but it was growing worse each day. It eventually came out that he had a long-term repressed anger towards his boss, which needed to be addressed. After undergoing a short course of acupuncture, taking *Milk Thistle*, addressing the situation with his boss and taking up running, the pain eased within a very short period of time.

Craving affects the heart

In TCM, excess craving and always wanting more is considered harmful to the heart. This is so common in today's pressured society where we have so many options available to us. In the past, men or women would be born into a village and their life path would be laid out for them. To survive, they would have very little option but to remain in the village, follow the profession of their ancestors and stay within the cultural restraints of society. They knew exactly what was expected of them. In modern society, however, we grow up with so many options available to us. We are told that we can be whatever we desire – astronauts, engineers, artists. We have choices about where we want to live, which religious beliefs we want to follow, which social opinions we support, etc. This surplus of opportunity comes at a price – stress. It creates an inner voice that is never satisfied, always demanding more than we can give. No wonder our society now has more heart disease! According to TCM, some of the physical symptoms that go along with this include palpitations, over-excitability, insomnia and restlessness.

There are many classical Chinese medical texts that warn against excessive desires. Leading a simple life and moving your focus to spiritual growth is the best remedy. In this way, breathing techniques, tai chi and qigong can be very useful. This does not mean we should be without ambition. There is nothing unhealthy about wanting more from life. Being hopeful about health, finances and relationships is in itself healing. It is the negative dwelling on the things that we don't have and not being satisfied with what we do have that is harmful. Keeping a gratitude diary where we note down all the little things we can be thankful for can be a powerful way to keep us from desiring more. This action of noting down the things that we are grateful for, such as having a family or even just having a warm place to sleep at night, can help to put things into perspective when we feel we don't have enough in life. Getting involved in voluntary community work also helps us move our focus away from what we want and need and can be very medicinal. *Craving Essence* is a good remedy to support treatment.

Worry affects the lungs and pancreas

Worry is unavoidable in the times that we live in, when there is so much social instability. However, for some people there are some pre-existing disharmonies in the body that could lead them to worry constantly, even when there is nothing significant to worry about. This type of person worries excessively about everything. In TCM, we expect this to adversely affect the pancreas and the lungs. The first physical signs usually include a stiff neck and shoulders, digestive problems, breathlessness and abdominal pain and distension. In the long term, it can also lead to asthma and other lung disorders. Because worry drains and robs the body of energy, it can also lead to fatigue.

There's a good exercise to do before bed in cases of worry,

especially if insomnia is also a problem. Cross the palms of your hands on your chest, take a few deep breaths (feeling the movement of your chest caused by breathing) then, during the next exhalation, sing the word 'aaaah' quietly to yourself, drawing this out as long as is comfortable. You will feel the vibration under your palms. Imagine your lungs as bright white while you do this exercise. Also, taking each worry (especially those over which you have no control) and offering it to God in faith can be very useful. Say to yourself, 'I now offer this worry [name it] to you God and trust that you will resolve it in the way it must be.' It is also vital to cut sources of refined sugar that further places stress on the pancreas and learn a technique such as Hara breathing.

Pensiveness affects the pancreas and heart

This is very similar to worry but involves constantly thinking about a situation, event or person. It's not so much worrying but rather brooding and obsessive thoughts. It will cause similar symptoms as worry and the same exercises for worry apply.

Sadness or grief affects the lungs and heart

There are times and circumstances where we will not be able to avoid sadness and grief. Separation or death from someone close to us leaves a gap and can result in one feeling lost. Long-term grief will lead to a weak voice, breathlessness, lung problems and weeping. It can adversely affect the immune system, leaving the person prone to infection. In women, it can even cause menstruation to cease. Repressed sadness over a long period of time, when tears are unexpressed, will, in the long run, upset the fluid metabolism. In times of grief, it is essential to have a good support structure that we can move closer to in order to fill the gap.

Fear affects the kidneys

The best example of this is uncontrolled wetting in acute fear and it is also often seen in children who are anxious about a family situation (bedwetting). Chronic anxiety can manifest itself physically with palpitations, insomnia and night sweating. Where patients suffer from chronic fear, they usually have a very pale complexion. Fear can also lead to chronic diarrhoea. In this case, acupuncture and some other remedies such as *Zincum valerianicum*, *Avena sativa* and *Stress End* can be very effective for those suffering from anxiety or panic attacks.

Guilt affects the kidneys and heart

Guilt may arise when people feel they have done something wrong or in those who always tend to blame themselves even if they have done nothing wrong. Symptoms that might arise from long-term guilt include an uncomfortable and unsettling feeling in the chest, abdominal pain and distension. Guilt is often also expressed as depression, which might result in a nervous breakdown or, in severe cases, lead to suicide attempts. There may also be a ruddy dark complexion and eyes that shift about rapidly. If there is guilt, the best remedy would be to talk to someone you can trust.

The Chinese organ clock, which can easily be found on various websites, explains when the best time is for 'maintenance' to be carried out on an organ. Just as a factory that runs 24 hours will shut down certain functions during a day for maintenance, our body does the same with the organs. For healing a particular organ, meditation is best done at the time at which the 'maintenance' on that organ takes place. Take a few minutes each day to meditate on that organ with some deep breathing. The best time to heal the gallbladder and liver is, however, during the night, but as one is not expected to wake up to do these exercises, care should be taken to be in bed by 10 p.m. and also to take a few drops of *Milk Thistle* just before bed. In addition, avoid eating heavy greasy meals before bed.

Acupuncture is an oriental form of therapy for many medical problems. This involves inserting fine needles into various active points on the body. Acupuncture appears to date back to somewhere between the fifth and third century BC. It began in China but soon spread to other oriental countries and in the past century it has also been practised in Europe. Acupuncture is based upon the principle of there being a continuous flow of life energy throughout the body. This force has two polarities that alternate rhythmically every twenty-four hours, flowing in paths. Meridians are traceable on the skin. On each meridian, there are acupuncture points that are stimulated by acupuncture needles, thus influencing the appropriate body organs, nervous system or affective area. The number of treatments varies, depending upon the nature of the illness or pain, how long you have suffered with it and your general state of health. Usually a patient begins to feel the benefits of acupuncture after the fourth or fifth treatment. Many people who have been helped may retain their improvement for months or for years. Those people whose symptoms return may be helped again with a few additional treatments.

Acupuncture can be effective in treating a wide variety of problems. Almost any painful condition may be treated with this form of therapy. It is also very successful when a patient is struggling to overcome emotional issues and associated problems, for example excessive consumption of alcohol, drug abuse and smoking. Acupuncture and laser therapy today are the most helpful combination in more chronic cases. Laser therapy, given under qualified supervision, can do no harm and is, in many cases, very successful.

There have been several studies conducted on the treatment of depression with acupuncture. One study carried out at the University of Arizona in 1998 found acupuncture to be very effective in treating depression. At least 70 per cent of the subjects experienced at least 50 per cent reduction of symptoms.

Acupuncture can be particularly effective when treating pregnant women who are clinically depressed or women who develop post-natal depression. Clinically depressed women who are pregnant face a dilemma because they are reluctant to use antidepressant medication that could affect the development of their babies. On the other hand, the chronic stress of depression can itself be detrimental to mother and infant. Therefore, acupuncture is especially recommended as a safe therapy during pregnancy.

With post-natal depression, action should be taken at the first signs of trouble, as it is a condition that can quickly spiral out of control. A capsule of zinc (15mg, twice daily) or the excellent homoeopathic remedy *Zincum valerianicum* can be of great help but so can acupuncture, and hopefully this will address the problem fairly swiftly.

In this chapter, I have tried to show that there are alternative ways of treating depression. I have serious misgivings about some of the strong medication that is prescribed for this condition and have tried over and over again to explain to people how important it is for them to rediscover a feeling of responsibility for their own bodies. However, it is always advisable to seek professional help for the treatment of depression, and it must be remembered that it can be dangerous to stop taking medication abruptly without the knowledge of the doctor who prescribed it. I have no doubt that any competent doctor or specialist will be only too willing to help sufferers of depression reduce their drug intake. It is important to remember that help is at hand and a lot of problems can be overcome if you accept you have a problem and ask for professional help.

EIGHT

Unhappy Relationships

SITTING IN a gloomy airport and still shaking from some news I had heard, I felt that there would be no better time to write this chapter. I had left it for as long as possible, as I found it quite a difficult subject to write about, and yet there are so many things that can make a relationship unhappy.

I had just heard some upsetting news about a patient of mine, and although I had tried to help this particular gentleman several times, I must admit that on this occasion I failed. The man in question was a lovely gentleman in his 60s. He was a religious leader with a large following, and it was evident that everyone loved him. He was married with children, and the marriage had been a happy one until at a certain point, even though he felt everything was going well, his wife unexpectedly refused him any physical contact. He began to feel inadequate as he tried to discover what was wrong. I suggested that I could talk to his wife, but she totally refused. The only explanation she could give was that she felt suffocated whenever he went near her.

He spoke to his doctor, who referred him to a psychiatrist. The psychiatrist could see what a nice man he was and felt sorry for him, but her only piece of advice was that he should consider having an extramarital relationship. He returned to me completely confused. When he told his wife what the psychiatrist had said, he listened in disbelief as she said that he should go ahead if he felt that way, as long as she did not have to hear about it. That confused him even more. He opened his heart to me one evening and told me that his religious beliefs would not let him do such a thing. Nevertheless, as time went by, these feelings of inadequacy increased, and, slowly, a relationship developed between him and one of his parishioners. He then began to feel loved and happy again. Although I thought he had come through the worst, and I had supported him through counselling and the use of acupuncture, I warned him that it was quite likely he would experience feelings of guilt and that he might end up needing further help as a result.

Sure enough, I saw him a few months later, and, although he was still quite happy, he had developed a massive guilt complex, and I felt the need to have a man-to-man talk with him. That was on a Friday. On the Sunday, he apparently preached the best sermon of his life, and the whole congregation was impressed with all he had to say. But immediately following that sermon, he went to the nearby river and drowned himself. Many were devastated by this tragedy, as was I when I heard the news, but after a long struggle with his conscience he finally reached the decision that he could no longer face going on with his life as it was.

I was sympathetic towards this man, as I could see the problems that he faced. It is all well and good to say that the Bible teaches self-control from Genesis to Revelations, but everyone has feelings. When these are difficult to control, only with the help of God can one overcome them. This unfortunate man probably fought his case just as King David fought his feelings of lust when he desired Bathsheba. But they both failed, though with different outcomes. In King David's case, he sent Bathsheba's husband to die on the battlefield, while in my patient's case, it was he who paid the ultimate price for his infidelity.

It seemed to me that the main cause of this man's problems was the difficulties he and his wife had in communicating with one another, and this is often the problem in troubled relationships. I have talked to hundreds of couples on the brink of a break-up in their relationship and have tried hard to reunite them. But bringing a couple back together is a very difficult problem to solve when those involved are no longer capable of communicating with each other.

An elderly couple who have been married for 30 years came to see me recently. Although they now manage to resolve any disagreements by sitting down and discussing them, this has not always been the case, and at one time, they had grown apart. They seemed to have forgotten the enjoyment they used to experience in each other's company. When I asked the man if he ever took his wife out to dinner, he answered, 'No', so I suggested that they spent more time going out together socially, for example to concerts. I devoted a great deal of time speaking to that couple, and, happily, they were reunited. A total breakdown in their marriage was avoided by their willingness to start communicating with each other again.

The days have long gone since my mother taught us, 'If you have made your bed, you jolly well have to lie in it.' In times gone by, there was the belief that you should stick together and work through any difficulties that arose in a relationship, but now, if things do not go well, couples often take the simple way out and go their separate ways. Moral values have changed, and in this permissive society, relationships break up far too easily.

I am sometimes surprised and also angry at how little effort people make while trying to mend a broken relationship. So much encouragement is given by those who lead by example, but when a relationship fails, impulsive action is often taken to separate, which is, more often than not, regretted later. It is important in any partnership to learn to get to know each other properly. This can take time, but unfortunately we are often impatient. My father used to say, 'Give time a chance. When it appears that everything is lost, give it time, do what you can, leave the door wide open, and, by doing so, things often resolve themselves.'

I remember a young couple who came to see me many years ago when I was still quite inexperienced in practice. Even although they had all the material things with which to enjoy life to the full, it was obvious how unhappy they were. Both were from good backgrounds, owned an expensive house and had beautiful children, and yet they sat in front of me fighting like cat and dog. They swore at each other and called each other names. I let them carry on for a little while before asking them the crucial question, 'Can you live together?' They answered, 'Oh, we have to. We are good Catholics, and there is no way out. We have to stay together, but we are destroying each other.'

We had a long chat and talked about life in general until they calmed down. As the woman had problems sleeping, I gave her some suitable remedies. I also gave the man some remedies to help control his overindulgence in alcohol. They had allowed things to grow out of all proportion and saw everything as dark and gloomy, so I asked them to consider taking a different approach. I wanted them both to make a list, putting on one side all the positive attributes of their partner and on the other side all the negatives. I then asked them to return the following evening at the end of my clinic, when I would be able to devote more time to speak to them and to discuss the positive and negative points on their lists to see if we could find a solution.

The next night they returned to see me. He handed me a list as long as my arm detailing all the negative points about his wife, but sadly it only contained a few positives. His wife took the first step towards resolving their problems by saying that she had started to make a list but stopped. She then turned to him and said, 'Although I would probably have a longer list of negatives about you, I am willing to accept you as you are. I want us to think back to the beginning of our relationship to the time when we really loved each other and try to reignite that spark.' That was the turning point in their marriage. He broke down and started to cry. After that, they managed to work things out and they are still together after all these years, living quite happily. When I occasionally meet them or give them a wave, I know they are still happy together because of that four-letter word – love.

Love overcomes so many obstacles. When you are able to rekindle those feelings of love for your partner, this will help tremendously in overcoming any difficulties. When you lose sight of that love because of circumstances, and you experience problems as described in the chapter on hate, and misunderstandings arise, then love goes. If we really love a person, do we consider all the problems that they have or do we focus only on the physical cosmetic things when we don't love them any more? Love is the greatest healer of all. With love, we can overcome any difficulty. It is just a matter of how to go about bringing that love back into your life when you have lost it. What methods are being used? That is where the ability to communicate openly with each other is particularly important, and we have to look positively at ways in which we can restore what we have lost. Often by overcoming such difficulties, our relationships become stronger and life becomes more meaningful than it was before.

All relationships have good times as well as bad, and we need to be prepared to take the rough with the smooth. As my mother often said, it is the making up after a stormy time that keeps a relationship interesting.

I remember the time when my father and I visited an elderly couple as they celebrated their golden wedding anniversary. The husband was quite a boring man, and I will never forget him telling us that during their 50 years of marriage they had never had a row and everything was hunky-dory. My father whispered to me that they must have led a very dull life! But when a relationship deteriorates to the point where there are more rough times than smooth, then it is important to get to the root of the problem and find out what is really going on.

A lady came to see me not so long ago and handed me a list on which she had written down her thoughts. I was taken aback when I read it, because I felt this unfortunate soul was really suffering, and I wondered what I could do to help. The note said that she had become overly suspicious about not only her husband but also about more or less everyone around her, to the extent that it had almost become an obsession. She had become very anxious and panicky, worrying about every little thing, and felt on edge and nervous most of the time. She then continued by expressing her fear of events that might happen. She became afraid of travelling or of any change, and was always dwelling on the worst possible scenario. Her positive thoughts had disappeared and been replaced by feelings of insecurity and a lack of confidence, which had caused her to become a total wreck.

I spent some time talking things over with her and came to the conclusion that this situation had arisen due to her husband's unreasonable behaviour. I asked if she thought he would come to see me so that we could have a chat together, and luckily he agreed. A combination of events had led to her condition, of which he was actually unaware. It became obvious to me that, as a result of her lack of confidence and the problems in their relationship, she had actually developed, through a hormonal imbalance, obsessive thoughts which then escalated into bigger problems. When we spent some time together to uncover these, and slowly put things into place, they both realised that they could not continue in this vein. Slowly, the understanding between them improved and they regained the happiness in their relationship that they had not experienced since they were newly married. Once again, improved communication was the key, but there was also the problem of a hormonal imbalance which we took care to address properly.

Hormonal imbalances, as I have described elsewhere in this book, not only influence one's health but also influence the way in which one deals with relationship difficulties. For a man, the most difficult time can be when he suffers a 'midlife crisis' and loses direction in life, while women sometimes need help around the age of 30 or 40 and particularly around the time of the menopause. Menstrual and premenstrual tensions then become so obvious that women can seem like Jekyll and Hyde characters, and this can spoil an otherwise happy relationship if left untreated.

We also have to consider the effect that problems in our relationships have on others. A young boy I knew well came to see me when his parents were experiencing problems in their marriage. They were not getting on well, and his father was behaving badly towards his mother. Everything was done to help repair that relationship, but it was impossible. The children were the victims, especially this young boy. He became very impatient with his father. He could not stand the arguments that took place and became very upset and anxious, which resulted in his having difficulty sleeping. He had also started to scratch his face, arms and chest until they bled. He was so miserable that his mother brought him to see me. After chatting to him for a little while, he started to open up to me. He told me a little bit about the problems at home and how he wished his father would go away so that they could have peace. The poor boy was in a terrible state and had become slightly hyperactive as a result. I was amazed to see how much the flower essences benefited him. He became calmer after taking *Child Essence*, *Mood Essence* and *Confidence Essence*, all of which helped to settle him tremendously.

It is not only our mental state that we need to keep a close watch on during troubled times in relationships. We also have to pay a great deal of attention to our physical health. When I carried out research in Holland on people crippled by rheumatism and arthritis, it came to light that many of the volunteers were victims of unhappy marriages, jealousies, resentment of work colleagues or breakdowns in communication. As I repeatedly say, human beings have three bodies – physical, mental and emotional – and we have to make sure that we keep all three of them in balance.

Romantic relationships are not the only ones that can be problematic, and one of the areas in which difficulties arise for many of my patients is the workplace. I remember a fine man who was the manager of a garage. His boss was a bully who never praised him. This worker had a sensitive nature and was a good father and husband, but at work he became extremely miserable because his hard work was not appreciated, even although he always gave 100 per cent.

His boss intimidated him and a breakdown of their working relationship followed. This caused the man to become very depressed. His hormonal system became imbalanced, and slowly he became a total cripple, making it necessary for him to give up work. In hindsight, however, that was a good thing, because he was forced to face up to the cause of his problems. When I treated his rheumatism and arthritis, he started to tell me about all the problems he had, and it was not only his mental health that improved by being away from that hostile environment but he also benefited physically and became almost limitation free. When his physical health finally returned to normal, I advised him that he could return to work but not to that particular garage. He managed to get a lighter job and was so happy that at long last he no longer needed treatment.

I used some wonderful remedies with him. As he had great difficulty in sleeping, *Passiflora* proved to be of tremendous benefit. I also used some homoeopathic remedies that were also of great help. We are still in contact, as he occasionally consults me over some minor ailments.

It is clear from this story and others that if something goes wrong or becomes imbalanced, we need to do whatever we can to find a solution or restore the balance. I regularly say to patients that the key to their recovery can be found within themselves. They have to face facts, recognise what is really going on and make sure that they get the balance right. For most of us, the majority of our waking hours are spent in the workplace, so it is important to realise that a problematic situation there is bound to affect one's health. One should do everything possible to re-establish harmony in order to enjoy life to the best of one's ability and to make the most of it.

It is important that we do a job that we really enjoy. Work

resentment is one of the most dreadful things that can happen. It sometimes only needs a tiny adjustment or one small word to reverse a situation, and by helping yourself you will also be helping others.

Some time ago, I could not understand why one of our clinics was not doing as well as the others. It had all the facilities to make it a good-going business, but yet the clinic was dull. Whenever I was there, I could sense an unhappy atmosphere. I then discovered that the two women who worked there did not see eye to eye. As it turned out, as a result of staff changes those two women left and two new employees came to work there. It was a delight to see the transformation as it unfolded. The turnover doubled. There was a happy atmosphere. Everyone benefited – the staff, through their salary, and us, as employers, through our improved business and the realisation that we no longer had to contemplate closing that particular clinic. The art of communication is vitally important in the workplace, and we must all aim to eliminate the negative and attain the positive.

Many young people today wonder what life is all about and what its purpose is. Life has a great purpose if we tackle our work and our responsibilities with love and devotion. Sometimes younger people, particularly students, find this difficult to accept. It is so easy to become depressed if we look at the state of the world today and the tremendous problems confronted by mankind. It then becomes understandable why relationships deteriorate.

Although it is quite easy to lose sight of the meaning of life, happiness is within reach of us all. We must reach out and grasp it, and even if it appears to be elusive and beyond our grasp, we must keep on trying.

I remember a teenager who came to see one of our physiotherapists. As she sat waiting, she started to cry inconsolably, and it took some time to calm her down. Through her tears, she told me that she had fallen out with her mother. One problem arose after another, and she felt it was probably best to make a clean break from her. To let her have some immediate relief, I gave her an injection of the homoeopathic remedy *Ignatia*. After a little while, she felt a bit better and managed to compose herself. We were then able to make a start to discuss her unhappy situation before her physiotherapy treatment. She had a very difficult life and needed urgent help. Not only had she fallen out with her mother but she had had a few unhappy relationships that had led her to experiment with all kinds of things. She told me that she was in a relationship, but that her partner began to drink heavily. As she depended on him, she tolerated this, but he then started to beat her up. She too started to drink heavily and lost her zest for life when he started to become even more violent. When he left, her neighbour who lived in the flat below came and empathised with her. She apparently had endured the same conduct at the hands of her husband until she finally got rid of him, and she now felt much happier living alone. The two found such comfort in each other's company that a close lesbian relationship developed between them. That made things even worse for my patient because she was not satisfied with this relationship, and it finally broke up. She was in a bewildered state, and although she no longer drank alcohol she started to turn to drugs. Her situation was quickly becoming uncontrollable, and her happiness was at stake. However, with the use of acupuncture and high doses of vitamin C, she was able to give up drugs.

Although the physiotherapist was able to help with her physical problems, she felt she needed some extra help to control her drug abuse. She cooperated fully with my advice and took a great interest in her dietary management. This was of great benefit to her, and with help from various sources the life forces within her were restored. She luckily regained her former health and is now enjoying life more fully than she ever did before. The lack of communication she had with her mother had been of great concern to her, but they were able to resolve their issues. She was fortunate to find a great man and she was able to turn her life around. As she said, there were several times in her life when she could find no purpose in living, and now she could see a happy future. A lack of confidence, insecurity and other negative emotions can all play a part in one's life, making one so confused that the negatives take over from the positives. When I see this patient now, I feel so pleased that she has regained her health.

Some years ago, a well-known psychiatrist brought his wife to see me. She was very depressed and the glimmer of hope in her eyes had gone. They came into my consulting room, and he began by telling me that he didn't believe in what I did but that maybe I could do something for his wife. To keep your own feelings under control in such situations is not always easy. I told him if he didn't believe in me, he should leave the room, as negative does not look for positive. Positive looks for negative and wants to restore it. I told him that a car will only run well if the battery is charged not with negative energy but with positive energy. He luckily agreed and left the room. Then, in tears, his wife poured out the long story of how she also had lost her purpose in life. She was an intelligent lady and had been happily married with lovely children, but as her husband was rarely at home she began to feel lonely. He was so absorbed in his work that he spent very little time with his wife, and what had previously been a happy relationship started to turn into one marred by discontent. He wanted her to take prescribed drugs for what he saw as her problem, but she refused and that made him angrier. In short, they were leading a terrible life. She thought that drink might help, but that only made matters worse. She then stopped taking pride in her appearance.

I felt I had to give her some hope for the future, so I told her that although she felt hopeless now, she was an attractive lady with a pair of beautiful brown eyes and a pair of wonderful hands, and there was a lot of work she could do. But I wasn't sure that I was getting through to her. There are times in practice that you sometimes feel inadequate and wonder what to do, but in this instance I was inspired to tell the lady the following story, which I have often mentioned since.

When our clinic was rebuilt, it needed additional parking. These parking spaces were created using layers of rubble and some tarmac. The same day as this lady consulted me, I was touched to see that a dwarf crocus had gathered enough energy and strength to work its way through all that rubble and tarmac to show its beautiful colour and life. I took her hand and said that positive would always win over negative. The enormous life force in a living thing – like that tiny bulb – has enough strength and power to work its way through the ground and show its glory. I said to her, 'That crocus is like you. You still have a life force within you. You can still do a lot to help others.' To cut a long story short, today that lady is the head of a successful business. We endured some difficult hours, but with counselling, acupuncture and the prescription of *Emergency Essence* she got through it all and taught her husband what life is really all about.

We hear such stories on a daily basis, and I could fill a whole book on the problems of separation, divorce and difficult relationships.

A beautiful girl now comes into my mind. She was quite happy, but, nevertheless, she came to consult me as she felt she might be showing signs of the onset of multiple sclerosis. After I carried out iridology tests and so on, I felt her concerns could be justified. I advised her to have this investigated and to ask for a scan or a lumbar puncture to be carried out. As she was worried, she decided on both. Unfortunately, these tests proved positive. She was obviously distressed but surprisingly got to grips with this situation remarkably well. Her fiancé supported her and we were able to make some progress. She followed the Roger MacDougall diet strictly, which I have written about in some of my books. She did everything to the letter, and, although it was a shock, I was surprised how well she controlled the whole situation emotionally.

Later on, however, she regrettably suffered a setback when some difficult family circumstances and other problems arose.

She then developed an infection on top of everything else, and a year or so later she was in a wheelchair. She again managed to cope remarkably until one morning she went to make some breakfast and found a note on the kitchen table from her partner. Although they had lived together for 13 years, he explained that he could no longer handle her deteriorating health and felt he had to leave. This had such a devastating effect on her condition that she was almost unable to do anything. I had some lengthy chats with her, prescribed *Avena sativa*, which is a great remedy in such situations, and also some *Confidence Essence* and *Emergency Essence* to get her on her feet again. After a long while, she was again able to cope with her condition. This amazed me because it was a very difficult situation. Not only had she depended on her fiancé for support, but she was also full of love for him.

I have said before that I am sometimes ashamed of my own sex because I have found over the years that women take relationships much more seriously than men. Often a man can opt out more easily than a woman and possibly feel stronger about the choices that they make.

Life overall is a great challenge and we often fail to take into consideration the feelings of others around us. This can have a terrible effect on our relationships, and, in the worst-case scenario, when these problems escalate they can lead to separation and divorce. If we are having problems in our relationships, it is very important to consider whether we might be responsible for the situation. Rather than running away at the first sign of trouble, we should remember that difficult situations can often be resolved if those involved are prepared to take responsibility for their own actions and to communicate openly and honestly with their partner. Don't be so quick to give up on a difficult relationship. Give yourself time to try to work things out and remember how powerful love can be when given a chance.

he became worried that one day his beautiful car would be taken away from him, and he could not stand the thought of that happening. So one afternoon when I went to see him for a friendly chat, I found him hanging above his car. It was a terrible shock to find him suspended there, and I then had to report this to the rest of his family who were in the shop. This distressing event left such a mark on my young mind and made me think about what life means to different people.

I heard of many suicides after that, and I was extremely shocked by the news each time. One day, my mother had been talking to a particular man shortly before he returned home to hang himself in his loft. Again, this seemed totally out of character for this gentleman. I just could not understand why people could do something like this. On another occasion, a local police inspector shot his wife during an argument and then shot himself. This caused such devastation in their family.

What brings people to the brink of suicide? What is the reason, I have often asked myself. Later on in life, I realised that it could be the result of some long-festering problems, inferiority complexes, family problems or certain hang-ups. The latter was the case with a young man who had consulted me a few times. He wasn't a homosexual but tended to feel more comfortable when dressed in women's clothes. He seemed quite a happy person. He had a lovely girlfriend, everything was fine, and nobody could understand why one day he dressed himself up in women's clothing and hanged himself, shocking the whole family. Did he take that action because he was seeking attention or was it because he could no longer conceal this habit that he had kept secret for so long? It is certainly not easy to understand what drives people to take such an extreme measure.

One area about which I have long had concern is the prescription of strong drugs that can have an adverse effect on patients and in extreme cases drive them to suicide. On one occasion, two ladies from Holland visited me in my clinic in Scotland to ask for my advice on how to deal with multiple sclerosis, as they were both suffering very badly with this disease. As we talked about life, one of the ladies told me that she had a very serious worry. Her doctor had prescribed her with a certain sleeping drug, which she took, but she told me that she became so depressed on that medication that she began to feel suicidal. I looked at the ingredients of this medication and found that it contained certain substances that could cause contraindications. When I investigated this a bit further, I found that that precise drug was believed to cause suicidal tendencies in some patients. I tried to warn the appropriate body about this, but it was not until many years later that action was taken. I asked myself again, how many trials are undertaken on drugs that we take or prescribe which are supposed to help the quality of people's lives? It took a long time before action was taken in that case, by which time that sleeping drug could have been responsible for many patients taking their own lives.

A lady came to see me not so long ago whom I had treated quite successfully for some other problem that she had previously had. She told me that from time to time she felt it necessary to take a certain drug to calm her down. It was a hypnotic drug, or tranquilliser, and I was worried about her taking this medication. I was so worried, in fact, that I advised her to ask her doctor if she could come off that specific drug, as I feel that with hypnotic drugs, unless they are absolutely necessary, one must be extremely careful when taking them. She tried to cope without this drug but found it difficult to wean herself totally off it, and then one day she felt a strong need to go back on it. Shockingly, one day she went outside and hanged herself from a tree.

As I take personal responsibility for my patients, I felt absolutely terrible on hearing this news. I felt I should have warned her more forcefully against taking this medication, but then it is extremely difficult for an alternative practitioner to give this kind of instruction, as we do not want to undermine the advice of a patient's traditional doctor. It is important for doctors to learn as much as possible about alternative medicine and of the remedies we have at our disposal to help people, as this unfortunate woman was really the victim of yet another drug that took away her self-control, and, in so doing, possibly resulted in her taking that fatal course of action.

Whenever I hear of a suicide, I try to find out what caused this person to feel such despair and to understand in what way our society is failing to help these people during their emotional turmoil. It is a subject I find difficult to address as, yes, I do agree that we have a right to lead our lives as we wish, but I do not agree that we have a right to take that life. When I am consulted by a patient who has suicidal tendencies, I often ask them to think of all those people who would have loved to have been alive today given the choice, for example the victims of the atomic bomb that fell on Hiroshima, where it is estimated that as many as 140,000 died as a result of the bomb and its associated effects. We should all appreciate that life has so much to offer and realise that negative thoughts can negatively influence one's life. Once again, we see the importance of having a positive outlook and of helping others who are struggling. We need to give them an opportunity to discuss their problems and find a solution rather than seeking to end it all.

A few years ago, I was consulted by a young man who bluntly told me that he was going to commit suicide. Once that thought is engraved in the mind, it can be difficult to dislodge, so I tried to get to the bottom of the situation and asked him what his reasons were. He said he felt life was so difficult; that although he was aware of the problems in life, there was very little he could do about them. People had cravings for money and power, and as a result they were involved in destructive activities; health-wise, there were many problems caused by increased toxicity and the manufacture of poisonous products that caused illness, and he said, 'We are so complicatedly created that I have asked myself, what is life? When I started to wonder what life is all about, I felt it was time to end it, because I could not see any future.'

This is a great problem for many people. It is important to realise that the future can hold so much for us all. The future can give us so much pleasure and joy if we can learn how to enjoy life and do all we can to overcome the negative. I asked him to visualise life as a mechanical machine. Sometimes it looks complicated and has to be repaired by the person who made the machine. It is possible to solve that problem because the manufacturer of the machine can give us an answer. However, the secret of life will never be known. Nature will always remain a great mystery to us.

I told him that my uncle, who held a responsible position in a psychiatric hospital, once took me to one of the wards and said, 'Here are people who want a real explanation of life. There are professors and scientists here, people with a lot of brains. Go and talk to them. You will find that you can have a good chat with them until they start to become totally confused and then get aggressive. Some are even so dangerous that they have to be cared for in a secure ward.' We all have to realise one thing in life, and that is that God has not given us enough brains to understand what life is really about. He has only given us sufficient brains to exist and make a daily living, but the mystery of life is far greater than we can ever imagine.

One way that we can perhaps gain a little bit more understanding is by following the laws of nature. We belong to nature, and, as Alfred Vogel always said, 'We are part of nature. When we obey nature, we then obey the laws of God.' This means that we should live as naturally as possible and not eat artificially created foods that can contaminate or destroy our bodies, as this is often where the problem lies. We often see that people's minds have become disturbed by an unhealthy diet, as in effect they have been poisoning themselves over the years. This can lead them to become chronically ill or, yes, even suicidal. When we have a problem with our health, it is important to look for the cause of the problem rather than take symptom-suppressing drugs, and we should also remember that the answer can often be found by taking an effective natural remedy.

There are many toxic and even poisonous substances which are today called 'remedies' and which are being prescribed on a daily basis. This worries me, just as in the case with the Dutch ladies and the sleeping tablets I mentioned. Everything in nature is in balance, as we see with animals and plants, but the minute that balance is disturbed then a natural reaction occurs. Only by correcting this can the balance be restored. I know we all want to be perfect in our work and in all we do, but this constant striving for perfection by unnatural means and through perpetual change will disturb the rhythm of life itself. We need to restore the balance in our lives.

When I spoke to the young man about these things, he opened his eyes and said to me, 'I think you have made a very important point there.' I was then able to share with him some pearls of wisdom that I came across in an old book written by a Welsh lady called *The Wisdom of the Cimry*. As I looked through this book, I came across some sayings that I agreed with. One was that the three beautiful beings of the world are the godly, the skilful and the temperate. The three attributes which are excellent for man to possess are valour, learning and discretion, and the three things that must be united before any good can come of them are thinking well, speaking well and acting well. The three things that are becoming for man are knowledge, good deeds and gentleness. There are three things that are everyone's duty to do – to listen humbly, to answer discreetly and to judge kindly. I was so encouraged by these sayings while writing this chapter on suicide, and this young man was also encouraged to look at his life anew and think about what he could change.

When I met my cousin some time ago, a professor, she was working very hard on matters of global affairs and she told me how much is being destroyed on our planet by man. I felt a little bit depressed myself while I was listening to her, but then I thought, 'Well, you are working hard to improve our planet, so surely we all can.' I told this young man that it would be more beneficial for him to become involved in trying to do something positive about life's problems instead of feeling suicidal about them. He should to try to help this poor world and to see how much man has got to live for. We have to do everything we possibly can to protect our world and preserve the wonderful nature that has been entrusted to us. Life is too wonderful to sit back and do nothing about it. We don't want to kill it. We want to keep it alive.

When people feel that they have come to the end of the road, action is necessary. Sometimes counselling is advisable, other times there is so much we can do with the many remedies available to us. Flower essences, such as *Confidence Essence* and *Emergency Essence*, can be of great help to turn our thoughts from suicide. Another remedy that can be most helpful is *Holy Basil Trinity Blend*, which I have described in the chapter on depression. I often find that this remedy, combined with *Avena sativa*, does a tremendous job.

I realise that when one comes to the end of the road and cannot see a way out, then self-destruction might come into the mind. We live in a selfish world, but we should find hope in William Blake's words, 'And we are put on Earth a little space, that we may learn to bear the beams of love.' There are so many things we can do to improve matters before negative thoughts take over our lives. Life can really be so beautiful if we focus on the good things in life and what life has to offer.

TEN

Forgiveness

FORGIVENESS CAN be a difficult concept for many people to deal with. As I have expressed in the chapter on hate, when you are consumed by this destructive emotion, it means that your problems are constantly at the forefront of your mind, and these negative thoughts can eat away at you. It is, therefore, much better to try to deal with the situation and eliminate the thoughts that cause this negative emotion. In some cases, people try to take revenge on the person that they hate, but this doesn't enable them to banish the negative thoughts from their minds. And revenge will certainly not help those who have health problems.

Forgiveness, on the other hand, is like a miracle. When negative emotions persist after a row or due to an unresolved dilemma, forgiveness can help to eliminate them. Positive will always win over negative. Forgiveness basically uses the same energy as a spiritual action. It comes naturally to us and strengthens the mind just as electrical energy strengthens the battery of a car.

About a year ago, a lady I knew fairly well came to see me. I was aware that we were both on the same level spiritually and that we were on the same wavelength, and she poured her heart out to me about the differences of opinion she was having with her husband. These were so serious that she had even contemplated leaving him, but the fact that she was so spiritually involved with her husband meant that she felt it would be impossible for them to divorce.

I had a long chat with her and spoke about the possibilities of healing the wounds that had festered through a great deal of misunderstanding and lack of communication between the couple. I told her that during the last century there lived not far from her current home an Irish hymn writer, John Martin, who wrote some very positive words. He had a deep understanding of what life was all about and how we should seek forgiveness. I quoted to her some words that have been very dear to me over the years when the matter of forgiveness has come to the fore. In one of his works, he said, 'Forgive as we forgive, oh Lord', and then the most important part, 'and set each other free'. These poignant words really sum up the point I am trying to make, because if we are able to forgive, we not only set ourselves free but we often set the other party free as well.

This lady went away and prayed hard, because a lot had happened that needed forgiveness. She managed to have a long talk with her husband and mentioned those words of the hymn writer: that if we can forgive, we will experience a deep sense of freedom. I see that couple regularly now, and they were reunited as a result of those words. I have often thought that if John Martin were still alive today, he would have been much heartened to learn that his poignant words have had such a positive influence on so many people's lives.

Forgiveness is an incredibly positive action and is characterised by love, peace, joy and the energy of truth. People often ask how we can promote this positive action, and I believe that if we can exhibit positive feelings, then these characteristics will emerge naturally.

I was reminded of this after the Second World War, during which I witnessed so much death and destruction in my homeland of Holland. When the war ended, we really hated the Germans for what they had done to our country and our families, and it took me a long time to get over the negative feelings that I had towards them. It was not until I went to Germany and carried out some lectures there that I realised that the German people were not monsters; they were people just like me, and this realisation allowed me to forgive and move on.

One of the most powerful stories about forgiveness I have ever heard was told to me by my friend Hans Moolenburgh. His aunt, Corrie ten Boom, was the daughter of a Dutch watchmaker who lived in Haarlem in the Netherlands. She and her family sheltered many persecuted Jews from the Germans during the Second World War. Sadly, however, she was betrayed, and Corrie and her sister Betsie were eventually imprisoned in the Ravensbrück concentration camp. Largely due to their maltreatment by a very cruel female guard, Betsie died, but Corrie miraculously survived the war and later gave a series of lectures around the world. One day, following a lecture in Germany, she was approached by a woman who admitted that she had done terrible things during the war but said that recently she had become a Christian and was seeking forgiveness for her deeds. She told Corrie that God would not forgive her until one of her former prisoners would forgive her personally. She then asked Corrie for forgiveness. Corrie immediately recognised the woman as the cruel guard who had been responsible for her sister's death. She stood rooted to the spot, and realised that she did not have it in her to forgive this woman whom she hated so much. Then she remembered the line from the Lord's Prayer: 'Forgive us our trespasses, as we forgive those who trespass against us.' Our own sins cannot be forgiven if we cannot forgive those of other people. So, not because she felt forgiveness but because she wanted to obey the scriptures, Corrie put her hands out and forgave the woman. It was only after she acted in such a way that she was flushed with real compassion for the former guard. Through that loving act of Corrie's she received greater love during her life and was a great blessing to others.

Love is such a powerful force in healing. We should never believe that we can cure anything; it is only God that cures through us. Spiritually, we can overcome a lot through prayer, meditation and positive actions. Physically, we can make ourselves stronger by including some of the many remedies that are available nowadays, such as *Valerian* and plant essences such as *Confidence Essence*, *Emergency Essence* and *Stress Essence*, all of which are extremely beneficial in promoting good health.

FORGIVENESS

The other day, a patient consulted me after she almost suffocated. It turned out that she was involved in a feud with her neighbour, and she was choked with anger. She relayed to me a long list of things her neighbour had done to her, some of which were horrific. I then asked her if she thought there was any point in carrying on with this dispute and making the problems worse. I asked if, instead, she would consider going to her neighbour to try to resolve their differences through talking calmly to each other. Initially, this idea horrified her, and she was really angry with me for even suggesting it. However, she returned about a week later and said she had been mulling over what I had said and felt that she should probably try to do as I suggested. She asked me for some advice on how she should go about it, and so I gave her several ideas. She later phoned me to tell me that she had put on a brave face and asked her neighbour if they could meet to discuss their problems, and she was pleased when her neighbour agreed. After a long conversation, they finally managed to sort out their differences. That was a very positive step in the right direction.

Sometimes people tell me that a certain act is totally unforgivable. But I believe that by looking more closely at problems, we can sometimes see that forgiveness is possible if we put in the effort to tackle the situation straight away before it has time to escalate into a seemingly insurmountable difficulty.

This reminds me of a lady who once came to me for help. She was in great need of work, and I helped her to find a job with a friend of mine. When she started, she was enthusiastic, but gradually her interest lessened. Unfortunately, her

133

time keeping became poor, she did not carry out her work efficiently, and there were other problems as well. I was asked if I could help by talking to her about her problems at work, which I kindly did. Nevertheless, my words fell on deaf ears and things went downhill. I talked to her again, but eventually she was told that she could no longer continue in this position. Despite the help that I had given her, she seemed to blame me for what had happened to her and developed a destructive attitude towards me. She made derogatory remarks about me to other people, which was uncalled for, and her comments were certainly not true. Whenever I saw her, she would turn her head the other way. Even though things went from bad to worse, I decided to do nothing about it. Then, one particular evening, I bumped into her. If looks could kill, I would not be alive today. I then thought, 'Enough is enough.' So I asked her how she was doing and took a genuine interest in what she had to say. She noticed that I was interested and this pleased her. The end result was that she embraced me. I was so pleased that my loving and kind attitude had managed to turn that whole situation around.

For no other reason than it was around Christmas time and I had to tell the staff a story, I decided to share that particular one with them. A few weeks later, one of my long-serving members of staff told me how she had had great problems with a lady she had once been friends with and that they both avoided each other like the plague. One day when she was beside this woman at the supermarket checkout, my employee remembered my story and thought she would turn the other cheek and speak to this person. After breaking the ice, the other lady then suggested that they went for a coffee together. The outcome was that their previously good relationship was rekindled.

As we have already seen in an earlier chapter, harbouring feelings of hate can have a detrimental effect on our health. Negative thoughts are so destructive. We must never forget that we are responsible for everything that we do. We all make mistakes and it is important to recognise that fact. If we are to take emotional responsibility, we must accept that, realistically, we cannot change a certain situation unless we show a little bit of love. It is so important to try to help the other party involved or even to accept the situation in order to restore a relationship.

This reminds me of the time when my youngest daughter got married. My friend, Dr Hans Moolenburgh, wanted to make a speech, but at the last moment he was unable to attend the wedding. He sent me his speech, however, and in it, as the bride and groom were both in the medical profession, he made reference to the importance of their jobs. He said that whether or not a doctor or therapist is successful in treating his or her patients often depends on how he or she sees their job. He wrote that he had met a lot of people in the healing profession, including some well-known medical professors, who knew so much that they became top-heavy and nearly tumbled over, and yet they were poor healers. He had also known some humble therapists with little knowledge, but they were able to heal people one after another. Knowledge, of course, is necessary, but what is that other imponderable substance that enters the equation? Therapist + patient = cure.

The best way that he could explain this was by telling a story from long ago about two brothers who lived in the Middle East. They were both farmers and also neighbours. One brother was married and had seven children, and the other brother was unmarried. They often had differences of opinion and didn't speak to each other for long periods of time. But one year, just after the wheat harvest, the unmarried brother could not sleep. 'Here am I,' he thought, 'with all that wheat, and there is my brother with eight more mouths to feed. I'll give him some extra wheat.' So, he filled two bags with wheat, and in the dark of the night staggered to his brother's barn to deliver them.

In the meantime, the married brother could not sleep either. He thought, 'There is my poor unmarried brother who has to go through life all alone. I will compensate for his loneliness by giving him some extra wheat.' So, in the middle of the night, he staggered to his brother's barn and delivered two bags of wheat.

Both brothers were much astonished when each discovered the following morning that the amount of wheat they had remained the same. They both thought that they had merely dreamt their good deeds, so that night they stayed awake and repeated their performance. Again, when they awoke, the amount of wheat in their own barns had not diminished.

On the third night, therefore, they each looked carefully around on the way to the other man's barn. So it happened that they bumped into each other on the border of their land. They understood straight away what had happened, dropped their bags and fell into each other's arms, crying, 'Brother.' At that moment, the Lord looked down from heaven and said, 'That is the way I meant people to behave towards each other.

On that place, I will build my temple', and Jerusalem was built on that site.

This complete and unconditional goodwill towards our fellow human beings is the real ingredient of healing and forgiveness. The negative to this story is the well-known tale of two Russian friends. As farmers, Boris asked Ivan, 'Do you love me?'

'Yes, you have always been my best friend. I do love you,' replied Ivan.

'Then if you love me, what is wrong with me, Ivan?'

'How should I know?' he asked.

'Then you do not really love me,' responded Boris.

As healers and practitioners, we need, apart from our knowledge, that basic love – not the love that says, 'If you scratch my back, I'll scratch yours', but the unconditional one, which, in the Bible, is called 'agape'.

The other story that makes this so much more meaningful is about a group of labourers in the Middle East who had to clear a field of its stones. When it became too hot to continue, they sat against a high stone wall to eat their lunch. The foreman assembled the different sorts of food the men had brought with them – one had bread, another had chicken and another fruit. He divided it all and gave it to the labourers. One day, one of the men had had to spend all his money on his wife who had fallen ill, and so he had not taken any food with him. The foreman quickly stood before him, shielding him from the rest, pretending to take something from his basket and said, 'Thank you very much. I appreciate that.' He had saved the man's face. It had taken him 30 seconds longer to reach his place again. Just before he arrived, a huge boulder fell from above and landed exactly on the spot where he always sat. It is said that this boulder had been especially created to kill the foreman, but it is the old story: if you go out of your way to do the unexpected good, you can even avoid death. So, this is the adage. If we are a blessing to all around us, then blessings will fall on our path.

It is often said that in order to forgive, you must forget, but that is not always possible. This reminds me of a lady who once consulted me about her unbelievably difficult and painful neuralgia.

After many years of suffering, she finally agreed to a facial operation, which unfortunately left her with a squint face and quite a visible scar. She consulted me in the hope that I would be able to help her with some cosmetic acupuncture, which indeed had some positive results. She told me that her family wanted her to sue the surgeon, but she felt that there would be no benefit in following this approach. She was not really interested in any compensation; she wanted help. She said, 'By the way, I have forgiven the surgeon.'

I said to her, 'But can you forget about what has happened?'

She said, 'How can I forget, when I look in the mirror and I am reminded every day what has happened? I have to live with it and carry away the experience as far as I can.'

I found this very interesting, as in the Dutch dictionary the definition of forgiveness is 'redeeming, forgetting and carrying away'. That is not always easy, but if one is able to forgive, it will free one's mind from a heavy burden.

ELEVEN

Eating Disorders

WHEN I wrote my very first book, 22 years ago in 1985, I expressed concern at the amount of media attention being given to the subjects of dieting and physical appearance. I was writing about the serious subject of anorexia nervosa, and my concern was that impressionable girls and young women were not being helped by unavoidable media images of thin models.

Sadly, today the situation has not improved. In fact, it is much, much worse. There are more glossy magazines, more television channels, more thin celebrities and, consequently, more pressure to conform to an ideal of physical perfection.

The two most common eating disorders are anorexia nervosa and bulimia nervosa, both of which are potentially lethal and must be taken very seriously. While they tend to affect mainly young women and teenagers, women of any age can fall victim to their perils, and men can also be affected.

Another major eating disorder is the over-consumption of food, resulting in obesity. This causes numerous physical and psychological problems and is becoming frighteningly common.

I am discussing these conditions in this book about emotional healing because they stem from an emotional source. I have heard it said that victims are abusing food in order to try to resolve an emotional issue, and I would say there is a lot of truth in this. In my work, I have certainly found it to be true in almost every case. Sometimes, however, unearthing the emotional issue, or issues, can be very difficult, and occasionally it is just not possible.

Anorexia and bulimia are both psychological disorders that focus on food consumption. Sufferers tend to have an abnormal relationship with food. Those with anorexia develop an inability to eat adequately and can starve themselves to the point of emaciation. They can have a distorted view of themselves, often genuinely believing they are fat when in fact they are disturbingly thin.

In the early stages, sufferers can keep their problem a secret and learn ways to avoid food without arousing suspicion As this condition progresses, however, it can be more easily identified because of the visible weight loss that sufferers undergo.

Those who suffer from bulimia, on the other hand, can keep their problem a secret much longer because their physical appearance can remain unaltered. This condition is characterised by abnormal cravings for food which result in binge eating followed by self-induced vomiting. It can also involve the abuse of laxatives and/or diuretics.

Both anorexia and bulimia tend to be what I call secretive diseases. Victims can go to great lengths to appear normal. Often worried relatives come to me and we go through lists of behavioural traits and other indicators to reach a conclusion that it is a possibility that their loved one may have one of these dreadful conditions. At other times, sufferers come to me as a last resort after years of conventional treatment involving doctors, psychotherapists, nutritionists and counsellors.

I do believe it is an area that deserves a multidisciplinary approach, and it is worth trying all forms of possible help. In my case, I have been able to help on many occasions with the use of homoeopathic and herbal remedies. In particular, I have found *Centaurium* to be excellent, because, as we have seen earlier, it is an appetite stimulant and improves digestion. Those who are underweight can benefit greatly from *NRV Food* from Abbots of Leigh.

I have noticed that those suffering from eating disorders generally conform to a certain type. Such people are often perfectionists, very intelligent and have a strong drive to succeed. If an area of their life suddenly plummets out of their control, they regain a sense of power by controlling their eating habits.

On one occasion, a smart, good-looking woman in her forties consulted me about an eating disorder. Having reached a certain level in her career as a lawyer, she had been bypassed for promotion, and this had hit her hard. Although she knew it wasn't rational, she formed the opinion that it had happened because she wasn't thin enough. She had tried to diet, and failure had driven her to feelings of total despair. She told herself she was not the type to fail, and certainly not twice in a short period of time. Realising that she couldn't reduce her food intake, she devised a plan to eat to her heart's content and then purge herself of her stomach's contents.

Her weight stabilised at an acceptable level, but she found that her habits didn't agree with her hectic social life, and she responded to an inner calling to seek help. Sometimes it can take a long time to help those with eating disorders, but fortunately in this case I was able to help her with some energy-balancing treatment and herbal remedies, which she responded to relatively quickly.

I do believe that the seeds of eating disorders can unwittingly be sown in childhood by loving parents. I have never forgotten the wise words of an old man who spoke to me when I was an impressionable teenager. He told me never to make personal comments about a person's appearance. Most personal comments, he said, are unnecessary, unhelpful and sometimes hurtful. I decided he was right and have followed this philosophy.

But even if adults know better than to comment on a child's appearance, it is very difficult to stop other children from doing so. We all know how cruel a truthful child can be. We can try to teach our children not to be hurtful to their peers, but it doesn't always work. And while most children can brush off being called names, it is the extra-sensitive child who will take criticism on board and be deeply injured. It is often difficult to recognise such sensitive children if they put on a front of being outgoing and confident.

Parents should, in my opinion, be careful not to place too

much emphasis on appearance with their children. And they should try wherever possible to shield their children from any insecurities the parents may have. It often happens that a child seems to absorb insecurities about physical appearance from a parent. For example, a mother who is constantly dieting and bemoaning her body can create a predisposition for such feelings in her daughter. I have seen it for myself many times, and I urge parents to protect their precious children from the fashion industry and all its foibles for as long as possible. Please carefully consider the value of allowing children and young teenagers to watch whatever television shows they want, as TV can have a very negative influence on them.

There were – and probably still are – cultures throughout the world where women eat to satisfy their hunger and accept their bodies as they are. I have met such people on my travels, and I can tell you that generally they are contented and feel valued in their communities. They live blissfully unaware of designer handbags and skinny jeans because they have no way of receiving such information. I wonder if television has reached them yet? Has it enriched their lives? There is no doubt that progress can be a positive thing, but, sadly, it can also have a downside.

Our world today is becoming increasingly competitive, and we have more choices than ever before. We must choose to be more discriminating, especially when it comes to protecting our young people. Too frequently I hear a young person saying, 'I hate myself' – we must turn this around.

Another situation that is a likely trigger for an eating disorder is when a person has suffered a personal attack or traumatic event, for example physical assault, rape, family breakdown or bereavement. How we handle such events depends a lot on first of all our genetic inheritance – meaning factors such as personality, constitution and disposition – and then on our current emotional stability. Sometimes families find it easier to understand why a member has an eating disorder if there is a plausible reason for it. If there is no immediately apparent reason, it can be harder to accept and can result in much soul searching on behalf of the parents. In all cases, however, the whole family usually suffers, and it can be heartbreaking to see. The one sentence I would advise any parent or friend to repeat often to a sufferer is: 'I will be there for you, no matter what.'

I would encourage anyone with any kind of eating disorder to learn the practice of visualisation, the secret of which is positive thought. My book *Realistic Weight Control* has a chapter on this subject. The subconscious mind will obey the conscious mind, and, used in the right way, this knowledge is a powerful healing tool. It is a question of imprinting the correct information on the mind. This is easy to do when one is in a relaxed state and the mind is receptive. It works – I promise you!

The basic method is to find a peaceful place to relax, then create a suitable daydream and enjoy it. For example, if you want to be more confident, picture yourself being confident in a variety of situations. Your mind is far superior to any computer, and most of us use only a fraction of our capabilities. This may sound like a simple technique, but it can have far-reaching results.

Now I come to another eating disorder, one which affects a

growing number of people throughout the world – that of obesity. This is the term applied to people who are overweight to a point that their health is suffering or will shortly begin to suffer.

There can be medical reasons for people becoming obese, but generally it is the result of overconsumption of food. In energy terms, food is measured in units called calories, and weight gain occurs when calorie intake is greater than calorie output. Yet again, we are aiming for balance. Indeed, balance is what our body's innate intelligence is constantly striving for within all its systems.

So why do people consume more food than they need? Is it just because the food is so delicious? Sometimes that can be quite true, but more often than not the basis for overeating is emotional.

One lady who consulted me was nearly 20 stones in weight when she squeezed into the chair in my consulting room. She begged for my help to make her thin again. I learned that she had had a hysterectomy at the young age of 26 and as a result was childless. She had been eating enormous amounts of food to fill the gap where a child or children would have been. This is a form of comfort eating and is all too common.

Simple dieting is not the answer. Some form of psychological therapy is required in such a case. There are many possibilities, and I helped that particular patient to find one which suited her. I was able to support this with dietary advice and natural remedies such as *Solidago Complex* and *Water Balance Factors* from Michael's. I also encouraged her to adopt a form of exercise that she enjoyed and to seek out new interests. She followed all the advice, and I am delighted to say that as she became happier, she became thinner. It didn't happen overnight and she had to work hard, but the end result was well worth it.

Our physical appearance is a great indicator of our general health and well-being. If we put on some weight, we should always ask ourselves why and keep probing until we find the answer. I know this is easier said than done in today's pressurised society. Perhaps we have introduced a new high-calorie food to our daily diet, or maybe we are too frequently eating a chocolate bar as a way of compensation for something. We must listen carefully to our bodies.

The world of natural health has a lot to offer to help the obese. One very useful remedy is *Helix Slim*, which was devised by my late friend and mentor Alfred Vogel. I urge caution when it comes to taking slimming pills, as they can be harmful with potentially dangerous side effects. There are, however, safe alternatives that can be helpful. For many years, having seen how traumatic it can be to be overweight, I have been working on the creation of a natural slimming capsule. And now, with the assistance of Michelle Mone, a well-known Scottish entrepreneur, the product, called *TrimSecrets*, is on the market.

Michelle had been unhappy with her weight for quite some time, and for over ten years she had tried various slimming clubs and diets, but nothing worked. By the time she came to see me, her weight had ballooned to 17 stone, and she felt so uncomfortable with her appearance that she was embarrassed to go out.

First of all, I helped her to focus emotionally and attune her mind to the task ahead. I explained about some new pills that I had developed, which she said she was happy to take, and she also agreed to adhere to my five-step plan for optimum results. She stuck faithfully to the plan, and the overall results were marvellous.

Michelle lost nearly five stone with the help of the capsules, dietary advice, exercise, drinking at least one and a half litres of water a day and taking time to relax. In fact, she was so enthusiastic about the capsules and the plan that she asked if we could market the product together so that it was accessible to all.

We did exactly that, and *TrimSecrets* are now widely available from health food shops and also on the Internet. Michelle is very happy: she got back her figure, looks fantastic and is very grateful for what I have done for her.

There is a word that is vitally important to all emotional healing, one which is relevant to everyone, no matter what their problem is, and that is nutrition. I cannot stress enough how important it is to ensure that our bodies are correctly nourished. For our mind and our bodies to function properly, we need a range of nutrients including vitamins and minerals, as well as the correct proportions of proteins, carbohydrates and fats. The food we eat affects our minds as well as our bodies. We all know that a piece of chocolate can be uplifting, but that doesn't give us a free rein to eat lots of chocolate! Again, I return to balance. It may sound boring, but a balanced diet is what we need. Sometimes it may be necessary to use dietary supplements to regain that balance, and if this is necessary, it is always advisable to seek expert advice.

I have long been concerned about the increasing varieties of junk food that are available and the effect that this has on general nutrition, particularly with regard to young people. Fortunately, however, there is also a growing awareness of the importance of looking after one's health, and this is serving to redress the balance a little. School food is becoming more wholesome, and exercise is being promoted.

I have helped many people who are depressed quite simply because they have put themselves on a very restricted diet in order to try to lose weight. In doing this, they are setting themselves up for failure and increased misery. Such behaviour can also lead to what is termed yo-yo dieting, where a person loses weight then puts it all back on, and the process can be repeated many times. This is actually very dangerous and interferes with the metabolism as well as playing havoc with the emotions.

A healthy appetite is indeed a blessing and I would encourage the enjoyment of good natural foods and a strong interest in cooking. Sometimes I find that people can be underweight for no particular reason. They tend to be people who are not particularly interested in food and take no great enjoyment from eating. This is just the way they are, but, nevertheless, they have to try to make sure they do eat enough and take in enough nutrients, otherwise they can develop health problems, like deficiency diseases. Osteoporosis, for example, is more common in underweight people.

Older people also can lose interest in eating, and this can lead to general feelings of depression. As a society, I would like to see a return to family meals being at the centre of life and the celebration of food generally. We seem to be growing away from this in northern Europe. Nature has blessed us with an abundance of things to eat and there is nothing better than a happy get-together over delicious food.

TWELVE

Hormonal Imbalances

EMOTIONAL STABILITY is becoming a rare thing. It seems to me that true contentment is becoming harder and harder to find in our modern materialistic world. And every day in my clinics I see patients whose hormones are in a state of total disarray.

Why should this be? I believe it is because the body's sensitive system of ductless glands – the endocrine system – is responding to a wide range of negative emotions and feelings, resulting in unpleasant physical symptoms.

The endocrine system is closely related to the body's energy system, and both are dependent upon the emotional health of an individual. This explains why some people heal quickly, others less so, and some not at all. There is truth in the saying 'You are what you eat', but the following is also true: 'You are what you think.' Every thought you have influences your body chemistry. The endocrine glands have a role in almost every, if not every, cell function and are pertinent to this book because of their sensitivity to the emotions – another reason why emotional healing is of paramount importance.

What exactly are hormones? They are chemical messengers, each with a specific role in the body. They are produced by a particular gland and then travel in the blood to the target site to do their job. This is a simple explanation of some very complex body chemistry.

The endocrine glands are termed ductless because they empty their hormones straight into the blood and not into a duct or tube. Glands involved include the pituitary, thyroid, parathyroids, adrenals, pancreas, ovaries and testes. We are talking about a very intricate system involving hundreds of hormones whizzing around 62,000 miles of blood vessels!

The main times in a woman's life when hormones can play havoc are puberty and subsequent menstruation, pregnancy, perimenopause and menopause. Men can also be victims of their hormones, and many report experiencing a form of midlife crisis. They tend to feel uncomfortable about getting older and can act out of character in an effort to regain the feeling of their youth. This has been labelled 'the red sports car syndrome', and while it can have a comical side, it has also been the cause of a lot of relationship break-ups. Generally, this subject is more out in the open these days, but it is still difficult to get men to open up and discuss their feelings.

The smooth running and synchronicity of all body systems are dependent upon hormonal balance, but sadly, as I have said, this is becoming increasingly rare. Negative thoughts and feelings, such as hatred, jealousy, fear and apprehension, result in blockages in the body's energy system. Energy is not able to flow freely. I suppose we could compare the situation to a traffic jam – just think of the congestion and problems they create. If the problem is not dealt with, physical symptoms manifest themselves and it is more difficult to re-establish the pure flow of energy.

This is why many of the problems relating to hormones, such as PMS and menopausal symptoms, are closely connected to the emotions. It is also a likely explanation as to why some women sail through all stages of life with very little, if any, discomfort, while others struggle and have a fight on their hands. There are other influential factors of course, like genes, lifestyle and diet, but people who are happy with their lives do seem to have an easier time of it. On the other hand, people often ask me why they are struggling so much while all their neighbours seem to be free from worry. I always point out that in many instances this is not likely to be the case. In today's society, with its preoccupation with maintaining superficial appearances, it is much more probable that a very large number of people, while appearing to be calm and in control, are in fact paddling very hard beneath the surface.

To be a health practitioner these days, one has to be a bit of a detective. There may be a pill for every ill (natural ones in my case), but it's not always so simple to find the right one.

I have seen it so often. A woman consults me with a relatively straightforward problem like, for instance, heavy periods. After all the usual investigations by a gynaecologist and various treatments, she is no better. She has tried everything. I give her herbal remedies and attempt to revitalise her energy flow with acupuncture. She improves a little, but I sense she is still stuck.

I use the word 'stuck' deliberately, because that is exactly what happens. A person has experienced a traumatic event, suffered a lot of hurt and been unable to move on with their life. They are not completely aware of being stuck, but they do have a vague sense of something not being right, and it is only after careful questioning that a conclusion can be reached. Often acknowledging the trauma can be enough to allow the energy to flow freely again, and with the back-up of various remedies true vitality can be restored.

There are many external influences on hormonal health, including the use of synthetic hormones like those in the contraceptive pill. Pesticide residue in food and water can also affect hormonal activity, as can polluting substances in the atmosphere. However, I am focusing here on the threat posed to our hormones and their delicate balance by emotional problems and particularly stress. I use the word 'stress' to cover the many trials and tribulations of modern life that have a negative impact on body, mind and soul. I believe it is a root source of hormonal imbalance, and when I am treating patients showing physical manifestations of such an imbalance, this is the best place to start looking for answers.

Since we are dealing with emotions and not just a physical problem, when a hormonal imbalance arises the matter should be looked at holistically: in other words, taking the whole person – body, mind and soul – into consideration. Stress has a direct effect on the hypothalamus and the pituitary gland, which in turn affects the ovaries and the sex hormones – oestrogen and progesterone. In fact, all the endocrine glands are affected in one way or another.

It is interesting that there are seven endocrine glands and seven chakras. Chakras are simply explained as energy centres that allow energy to enter and leave the body. Some people visualise them as like whirling windmills (very appropriate for a Dutchman!).

Each chakra is associated with specific organs and emotional states, as well as a colour. For example, the thyroid gland, which controls the body's metabolism, is affected by emotions like frustration and stifled ambition, and it is governed by the 5th chakra, which covers the throat area. This is interesting if you think that one way a voice can be stifled is if there is pressure on the throat from an unwelcome hand, and the throat is the site of the thyroid. The thyroid gland is very sensitive and can be negatively affected by traumas like divorce and bereavement or by unhappy relationships. So, if your thyroid is playing up, it might be pertinent to ask yourself who or what is stifling me?

There are therapies, including reiki, which work with the chakra system. Reiki involves drawing down universal energy and guiding it into the chakras in order to release any blockages and allow the windmills to spin at optimum speed. Some reiki practitioners claim they can feel a sensation in their hands when they encounter an energy blockage.

As far as the flow of energy is concerned, I understand this very well, because when I use acupuncture I am working with energy flow. And while I have seen acupuncture release many, many people from a particular pain, I don't always know if that pain had an emotional origin. It is not always the case, particularly with sports injuries – the business of energy flow certainly holds many mysteries.

As well as seven endocrine glands, there are also seven layers of light in the retina of the eye, and, furthermore, there are seven colours in the solar spectrum and seven scale steps in a musical octave. All these groups require harmony for happiness and health. If just one endocrine gland is out of step, harmony is lost, and the symphony will not sound pleasing.

Another therapy that can have a positive effect on the workings of the endocrine system is reflexology. This therapy is based on the principle that there are reflexes in the feet that relate to different body parts, and, by using various techniques with the fingers and thumbs, a reflexologist can pinpoint areas of congestion and use gentle pressure to provide relief. This relief extends from the point on the foot to the related body part and, again, releases blockages in energy flow. I believe that reflexology is an excellent way to exert a positive influence on the endocrine glands.

The use of essential oils from plants to create harmony for mind, body and soul is yet another way of restoring balance to the hormones and relieving the symptoms of stress and anxiety. Interestingly, some people believe that the potent essential oils are the hormones of the plant. Whether or not that is true, they are certainly a welcome gift from Mother Nature that can be put to wonderful use in restoring the body's equilibrium. The main therapy involving the use of essential oils is aromatherapy.

Another good treatment for hormonal imbalance is that of cranial osteopathy. It is especially useful in assisting the pineal and pituitary glands, as they are embedded within the skull. Any cranial misalignment, however slight, will affect these glands.

I remember one lady who consulted me with severe menstrual symptoms. She was surprised when I diagnosed a dislocated jaw and proceeded to correct the problem with manipulation. I explained that with the misalignment corrected, her hormones would rebalance and return to the correct level, giving her subsequent relief from her debilitating symptoms. Indeed, this happened, and she was delighted.

In my book *Menstrual and Premenstrual Tension* from the *Well Woman Series*, I describe the many ways in which I have successfully treated this condition with the use of remedies and therapies. I also explain that while the activity of hormones affects the mood and emotions of a woman, these very same emotions can affect the behaviour of hormones. It is a catch-22 situation.

Premenstrual tension is undoubtedly the result of hormonal imbalance, and it can cause a whole host of unpleasant symptoms and feelings, including anxiety, depression, lack of concentration, confusion, headaches and fluid retention. Amongst my patients, the most frequently mentioned symptoms are those of emotional imbalance, like inexplicable mood changes, depression and bouts of crying. In such cases, I recommend *Female Balance*, a remedy from Enzymatic Therapy that was created by myself and my son-in-law, Marcus Webb. *Female Balance* provides essential vitamins and minerals that are depleted in women who experience premenstrual tension. These critical nutrients are combined with concentrated extracts of herbs that women have depended on for centuries, such as Dong Quai, Liquorice Root, Milk Thistle, Black Cohosh and Chaste Berry.

Pregnancy is a time of great joy, but there are also conflicting emotions as the hormones dance a little out of tune. It is of interest that some women feel overriding happiness and positivity during these important nine months, while others are very weepy and depressed. Again, the power of positive thought is very important, but this can be easier for some than for others. Also, it is a time for a woman to be indulged, in my opinion, and again this is practical for some but not for others. There are often financial constraints that mean a woman has to keep working hard when it would be better for work to take second place to relaxation. People are all different, and some women feel more fearful about the process of giving birth. Some have supportive partners and families, while others are lacking in this very vital department. I have found the use of flower remedies, which work on a gentle vibrational level, to be supportive during pregnancy.

After the birth, it can take time for the hormones to stabilise, since they are most certainly dancing furiously at this time. Again, support, both from professionals and family, is extremely important, and there are also a number of herbal preparations that can be helpful, such as *Evening Primrose*. When there has been trauma, I sometimes prescribe *Arnica*, and in cases where there is a little bit of nervous anxiety, the excellent flower remedy *Relaxing Essence* can be beneficial.

Relaxing Essence is a wonderful product made from a combination of helpful ingredients and I thought it might be of interest to some readers to see what goes in to such a remedy:

Impatiens: Helps ease frustration, snappiness, irritability, agitation, nervous indigestion and tension. Impatiens can discourage argumentative traits that make life seem like a constant battleground.

Mullein: Balances the energy systems of the body, blocking out unnecessary thoughts so that it becomes easier to concentrate.

Dandelion: Allows the body to relax physically, gives effortless energy and the ability to 'go with the flow'.

Mimulus: Helps with everyday fears and anxieties, for example, job insecurity, fear of getting things wrong, anxieties over money or family and relationship problems, public speaking, health etc. This essence brings comfort, courage and security, making it easier to tackle the difficulties of daily life.

Elm: Helps the patient to quickly return to optimum strength but with a wiser attitude. It brings the ability to prioritise and see problems in their proper perspective, making it easier to balance home and work without overloading oneself.

Aspen: A remedy for fear symptoms such as apprehension, terror of impending disasters, paranoia, panic attacks. This essence helps the fear and apprehension lessen, allowing inner confidence and trust to grow.

Oak: Helps patients learn to pace themselves, set boundaries, delegate, understand limits, and act with patience and common sense.

Hornbeam: This essence brings a lively mind, a cool clear head with a renewed interest in work and life.

Bluebell: Helps you to hold your own, to get along with others and accommodate their differences in situations you would normally find difficult. This essence brings stillness, calm and tranquillity.

Verain: Ideal for people with demanding occupations, or people living on their nerves, who may overwork and suffer from a variety of ailments caused by stress and information overload. This essence will give them the ability to step back when necessary, relax and use their energies more effectively.

Also in the *Well Woman Series*, my book entitled *Menopause* explains the changes that take place in a woman's body at this time and offers common-sense solutions based on natural medicine. Some lucky women barely notice the menopause, but the majority have some new experiences to deal with. I have noted that those lucky few who sail through easily are usually those who pay particular attention to their diet, to optimum supplementation of nutrients, who exercise regularly and are not overweight. But these factors alone do not guarantee a smooth passage, because, as I keep stressing, the emotions are once again highly significant.

In Chinese medicine, the menopause is looked at as a blood-deficiency problem and focus is placed on treatments like acupuncture and cranial osteopathy. These help the system to regain balance and alleviate many symptoms.

I am often asked about HRT (hormone replacement therapy), and I have to say I have grave reservations about it. I believe that it is not suitable for women of a nervous disposition and also those who have thrombosis, fibroids, endometriosis, diabetes or gallbladder problems. In my opinion, there are still too many unanswered questions about this treatment, and I devote a whole chapter to this subject in my book. I remember back in the 1980s, when Gloria Hunniford and I did our monthly radio programmes, we often said, 'If you can treat a problem naturally, then do it naturally, because you never know where taking HRT can lead.'

Among the many natural alternatives to HRT is an excellent one called *Phytogen* from Enzymatic Therapy. *Phytogen* is a unique combination of phytoestrogens and vitamin E. The important compounds in this formula include vitamin E (essential nutrient for cardiovascular function), flaxseed oil (rich in lignins, which may be linked to the sex hormones), gamma-oryzanol (obtained from rice bran and has been studied for its relationship to cholesterol levels) and pumpkin seeds (rich in essential fatty acids and sterols. Essential fatty acids are known to be vital for sexual gland functions).

Phytogen also contains soy extract that is known to contain natural plant hormones. It is interesting to note that for thousands of years people in Asia have eaten a diet rich in soya and it is a fact that Asian women rarely experience the menopausal problems that Western women do. There is not even a term for 'hot flushes' in the Japanese language.

I have seen many women benefit from this wonderful remedy and others such as *Female Balance* and *Menopause Factors*.

There are also many herbal remedies that help menopausal symptoms. *Menosan*, made from sage, for example, appears to have a balancing effect on the hypothalamus, which can become overactive at this time of life as it tries to regulate fluctuating hormone levels. By regulating the function of the hypothalamus, *sage* has a beneficial effect on the sweat-regulating mechanism housed in the same part of the brain, making it useful for hot flushes. It may also help men who sweat profusely.

Among other herbal remedies that help with hormonal imbalance during the menopause are: *Dong Quai, Siberian ginseng, Agnus castus* and *Hypericum Complex*. I created *Female Essence* specially to assist with balancing the hormones, and it also helps with general emotional balance. I have also devised a special formula including *Evening Primrose* which is particularly good for this stage in life, because this is when essential fatty acids are needed more than ever.

Relaxation is very important in assisting the endocrine glands in their bid for balance. I advise fitting a special relaxation time into every single day. This need not take too long, but it cannot be rushed. It must be treated as a priority. Simply find a quiet, comfortable, safe place to lie down. Try to make sure you will not be interrupted. You can play gentle music if you wish, then lie down and consciously relax. Breathe in and out by moving the stomach and concentrate on this area. The hypothalamus particularly benefits from breathing exercises.

Some people respond well to the use of affirmations, and this can be an ideal time to use them. An affirmation is simply a positive message to yourself that you repeat either out loud or internally. Some people write them on a little card and put it in a prominent place so they see them often. Perhaps you could write: 'I am perfectly happy and contented with my life today', or 'I am at peace within myself and with the world.' This kind of message, when reinforced, is calming to the mind and can be of great benefit.

I cannot emphasise enough that the years around the menopause are a time for a woman to really take charge of her life and do whatever her soul yearns for. In classical Jungian psychology, 'soul loss' occurs mainly around the midlife period. Some women in this age group have told me they have felt a calling to be creative, perhaps to play music or write poetry. It is healing to respond to such a calling, and, in this way, the soul can be revived. Obviously, such ideas are open to interpretation and different people have different opinions, but I certainly feel it is a time of discovery.

Almost all women spend a lot of time caring for others, whether for children, other family members or work colleagues. This can be fulfilling, but there is often a yearning deep within for some time to follow the dictates of the soul. These can be major or simple, but, whichever, they are usually meaningful and can make a huge difference to the general vitality of an individual.

I have heard this time described as a period of emptying, when a woman decides to clear out the 'rubbish' from her life and start afresh. This sounds drastic, but it can simply mean she refuses to be treated as a doormat, or she changes job or moves house to embrace a simpler lifestyle. I would encourage this, because positive changes only serve to strengthen the life force and encourage hormonal balance. It is a way to assist emotional healing and pre-empt potential negativity relating to feelings of a loss of attractiveness and general ageing. Many women feel they lose their looks as they grow older, but as a man I would counteract that by saying that what they lose in youthful bloom they gain in character, and this is very appealing.

I would urge women to listen carefully to their body and soul. If you feel like shouting, 'Stop the world, I want to get off', do just that. It is your right to become quiet and contemplative and to retreat from the world. You will soon feel ready to return. Some women actually take a sabbatical for as long as a year to follow their dream. This, of course, is not practical for most people, but who can't manage a few hours or a few days?

It is also a time when many people start to search for meaning in their lives and can turn to spiritual comfort. This, of course, takes many forms and each can find what suits them best.

It is about this age that women realise time is not on their side and they don't want to waste a minute! The years ahead can spell freedom from the many constraints that younger women have – children, monthly periods, career building and so on. With a positive mind and a healthy body, the future can be most enticing.

There is a new, natural, progesterone cream, which can be very beneficial when trying to correct hormone imbalances. A great friend of mine called Sally Longden, who works for a company that produces *Naturone*, a specific brand of progesterone cream, was able to give me a lot of information about this product.

She explained that:

> Progesterone is one of the first hormones in the steroid pathway. It is called the mother hormone because so many other hormones are derived directly from it – the corticosteroids, the stress hormones, one pathway to women's oestrogen and men's testosterone. If the basic hormone is lacking, then this will cause deficiencies in all the hormones mentioned above . . .
>
> The most wonderful aspect of natural progesterone therapy is that it is natural, i.e. it is the bio-identical molecule to the progesterone molecule produced in our body, it is *real* progesterone. By applying natural progesterone, we are merely filling the reservoir of the mother hormone and thereby allowing the body to balance and heal itself. Our bodies are amazing healing machines – give them the basic fuel they need and every cell, filled with innate intelligence, will respond by producing new, healthy cells. Within a short period of time, we have new, healthy organs and a state of optimum health.

Sally emphasised, as I have also done, the health problems that are being caused by the increasing number of toxic chemicals that now exist in our environment and argued that these are causing hormonal imbalances and compromising our immune systems. She calls these chemicals 'endocrine disruptors' and believes that:

Many of these endocrine disruptors are now mimicking oestrogen. They are called xeno-oestrogens and come from petrochemicals and pharmaceutical drugs. In our homes, we are exposed to them on a daily basis, in our foods (synthetic hormones in our meat, pesticides and herbicides), the creams we put on our skins, all the chemicals we use to clean our houses and the solvents and paints we use.

To survive this new environment that we, man, has created, we are going to have to use our brains, take responsibility for our health and give our bodies all the help we can in order to restore the balance. We need to increase our nutritional intake, especially with the antioxidant nutrients, to neutralise free radical damage, and we need to keep the xeno-oestrogens under control with progesterone in order to restore hormonal balance.

Oestrogens are a very potent class of hormones. The only antagonist to oestrogen is progesterone. One of the worst characteristics of oestrogen is that it switches on a gene called the BCL2 gene (a cancer gene). This then causes the cells to multiply; they do not differentiate and they do not apopoxis (die). If this condition is unopposed or [is not] balanced by adequate levels of progesterone, it can then lead to a cancer tumour, if the immune system is compromised. Progesterone switches off this BCL2 gene and switches on a protective gene, the P53, which gives the right message to the cells. They then mature, differentiate and die and are thereby replaced by other healthy cells . . . When oestrogen is not balanced with its antagonist, progesterone, it gives rise to this dangerous state of unopposed oestrogen which, in turn, produces many distressing symptoms referred to as 'oestrogen dominance'. These vary from PMS, infertility caused from endometriosis, fibroids and polycystic ovaries and, of course, the low sperm count in men (that has fallen 50% in just 50 years) to increased cancer risks, depression, heart disease, gallbladder problems, thyroid problems – to mention just a few.

Sally was also able to point out a very interesting link between progesterone levels in the body and stress, which as I have already discussed, is a major problem in modern society:

Adrenalin, noradrenalin and cortisol (one of the corticosteroids) all come directly from progesterone. We now demand outputs of stress hormones never experienced in our history before. We have become adrenalin junkies – producing it all day long, when we drive a car, watch scary movies, [conclude] business deals, dive out of aeroplanes, etc. As it is the survival hormone, our body will produce it before any other hormone. Consequently, due to the high demand, our progesterone levels are sucked dry, leaving not enough to balance the rest.

Cortisol, likewise, is a drain on our progesterone levels, as this is the hormone produced when we worry – a national pastime! Deficiencies in the other hormones then lead to early degenerative disease – a lack of the corticosteroids results in increased allergies, autoimmune disease and inflammatory conditions, arthritis, etc.

Finally, Sally told me about the benefits that progesterone cream could have in treating osteoporosis as: 'Apart from balancing oestrogen, progesterone is the only known chemical, natural or otherwise, that stimulates bone-building function, thus being very beneficial in the reversal of osteoporosis.' This benefit is not restricted just to women but can also be experienced by men, more and more of whom are being diagnosed with osteoporosis these days.

Thus we can see that natural progesterone cream could be an answer to many of the problems that have resulted from our hectic modern lifestyles.

As I conclude this chapter, I would like to encourage you to make friends with your hormones and embrace change in your life. Empower yourself with knowledge and accept support. There are no prizes for going it alone. And remember, if the power of thought is so powerful, the power of positive thinking must be incredible!

THIRTEEN

Loneliness

LONELINESS IS an overwhelming emotional state in which a person experiences deep feelings of emptiness and isolation from the world. It is not only when a husband, wife, partner or a best friend leaves that people can feel very lonely, and you don't need to live alone or have no family – there can be different causes and degrees. The old saying that you can feel lonely in a crowded room is very true. Many of those who consult me with such problems lead an active social life, have a family and a demanding career. It is about more than just wanting company, and most of us will experience this feeling at some time during our life. Loneliness can happen to people in every profession, economic, ethnic or age group.

Those in the midst of dealing with this painful emotion tell me how miserable they feel: they believe that nobody seems to care about them, that they have no friends and that their life is ebbing away. I meet people like that every day. I listen to them intently, because I know how isolated they must feel and often, when they reach old age, how they can end up sitting in a small room by themselves just waiting to die.

In their advanced years, many elderly people lose their loved ones and friends, and when they experience illness and perhaps disability themselves, they can feel like prisoners in their own home. I witnessed this loneliness in the elderly as a child when I used to visit my aged grandmother. It was obvious that many people in the nursing home where she lived were lonely, and for many years as a boy I visited a lady there who often cried through loneliness but then looked forward to my Sunday visits.

An elderly lady sat before me in tears the other day. She had been calling out for help from her priest, her neighbours and from people she thought of as friends. Day after day, she told me, she sat there in her house, becoming more and more lonely and miserable, with no positive outlook. She then told me how she had developed an itch all over her body, and I instantly knew what was wrong. The liver, which filters 1,200 pints of blood in 24 hours, becomes disturbed during emotional upsets. When problems relating to the emotions cause such despair, an awful itch can develop and sometimes appears as redness on the skin, as if the body is crying for help. *Milk Thistle* can be extremely helpful in such cases, or sometimes prescribing *Ginkgo biloba* to patients will give them a lift.

Being able to contact a sympathetic organisation can also bring about a lot of relief when trying to cope with loneliness. We sometimes see that when people no longer feel able to phone someone for help or to turn to the Samaritans, they end their lives, and that is so sad.

I sometimes feel we are becoming more and more lonely in today's society. The particular stresses we face in modern life tend to make people more susceptible to loneliness. We are so geared up for our busy lives at work, making more money and attaining more material possessions, that we forget about straightforward human relationships. Then, when we have to take stock of what is important in our lives, it can hit us hard when we realise that we are alone.

A hospital consultant asked for my help some time ago. I felt deeply for him, as I could see straight away that he was a caring person. He had helped thousands of people through their agony and problems until, unfortunately, he made one mistake with a patient. The newspapers and the media can be so judgemental, and when they reported this story to their readers and listeners, they blamed him for something that he could not have foreseen. He told me how he now felt so lonely because he used to lead such a fulfilling and busy life. He had been at the top of the ladder in his career and now felt his life was empty. I asked him how many of the thousands of people that he had helped over the years had been there to offer him support and comfort during his time of need. To my shock, he said there had been no one. I felt deeply sorry for this gentleman, because I know he had done so much to help others, and yet when he needed help, no one was there and he felt very alone.

Similarly, some time ago, I paid a visit to a consultant whom I regard as one of the best medical consultants I have known in my lifetime. Unfortunately, he now suffers from senile dementia, and when I looked at him and recalled what a brilliant mind that man once had, I was shocked to see that he had ended up so alone.

When someone sees no hope for the future, he or she can become particularly lonely. We probably don't realise how much of a lift it can give lonely people if we take the time to visit them and show them how much they are thought of. But in today's world, sadly, many people are of the opinion that 'As long as I am all right, Jack' everything is fine, and they don't take enough time to think of others around them. The other side to this coin is that when they need help, they can find themselves with no one to turn to.

We shouldn't underestimate the despair that loneliness can cause. A young girl came to me not so long ago. She was inconsolable and needed help. 'My partner has left me and I feel totally alone,' she said. 'I am heartbroken. I don't know what to do.' I could see how distressed she was and tried to help her in every way possible, but to no avail. She was actually a person who, to all intents and purposes, was dying of a broken heart, and in fact that was what ultimately happened to her. Isn't it awful to think that a broken heart can actually lead to death? We have to realise that there are people in this world who need human help and understanding, and we have to try to find out how we can love our neighbour as ourselves, as I have already mentioned.

There is a man in the Old Book called Job who had everything at one time in his life, then, slowly, he lost the lot. Nearing the end of his life, he declared that God 'stretches out the north over the empty place, and hangeth the earth upon nothing' (Job 26:7). He then went on to say, 'These are the fringes of his ways; and how faint a word we hear of Him! But His mighty thunder, who can understand?' (Job 26:14). He felt alone but when he came to the bitter end and asked for help, help appeared.

We all need to have hope for the future. When I speak to my Creator, I know that there is help for every lonely soul. But we all have to try to understand the needs of other people and do whatever we can to help them.

People do not share as much as they used to. In times gone by, when people were in need and poor, there was much more sharing than there is today, even though we now live in a world where many of us probably have more than we actually need. I once read that there were three things that are lovable in man, and those things are peace, wisdom and kindness. I often feel there is not enough kindness around. We use the expression 'Give and take', but too often that 'take' has become the most important part in one's life. We should remember some other important sayings: 'We reap what we sow' and 'We get out of life what we put into it.'

A young man I saw a few years ago comes to my mind. He was a very promising footballer but suffered a serious injury and was worried that his career was about to come to an end. I could see that he was lonely in his battle, and although his fiancée supported him, he did not know who to turn to for help. His manager told him that he was no longer fit to play, and he felt he would be pushed aside for other players. Fortunately, he quickly improved following a course of acupuncture, some *Joint Mobility* made by Michael's and *Arnica gel*. He recovered and went back to play as well as he had done previously. However, he still felt lonely in the battle he had with his manager, who eventually sold him to another club. We became quite friendly because I did everything I could to help him, and he was able to continue in his career as I was able to prescribe natural remedies that helped him overcome his physical problems.

So yes, we might be lonely and, yes, we might be disappointed in friends whom we expect to be there during our lonely times, but we can still find a friend in nature.

My relationship with this wonderful friend started when I was very young. In those early days, when I cycled through the fields in Holland during the war, I would hide from the Germans under one of her beautiful coats. Whether it was spring, summer, autumn or winter, all her coats were lovely. She has been with me throughout my life, and when I go to her with a problem, she is always there to listen and give me advice. She is a princess. What a wonderful gift this is in times of loneliness when we have problems, where we can talk to her and she gives us guidance.

While writing this book, one of my oldest and dearest friends is battling the last enemy – death. Whenever I visit her, I am aware of how lonely she feels. Although I can see in her eyes how difficult things are for her, they still give a little glimmer of happiness when she is surrounded by friends and those who care. She was a music teacher, and I have listened to the sound of her music. She is in harmony with herself and her Creator. Looking at her friends, who surround her with a lot of love, I ask myself, 'Is this not what real friendship is all about?' We shall discuss this in the next chapter.

FOURTEEN

Friendship

MY VERY good friend and mentor for over 40 years, Alfred Vogel, said in many lectures that love is the most powerful emotion in the universe. I agree with him. Life becomes more meaningful when love is part of it. We all know that if we love someone really deeply then we are blind to their imperfections. Love conquers all. It is actually the only commandment in the New Testament of the Bible. In Matthew 22:36–40, when asked by one of the Pharisees, 'Teacher, which is the greatest commandment in the Law?', Jesus replied, 'Love the Lord your God with all your heart and with all your soul and with all your mind.' In my opinion, this is the first and the greatest commandment. And the second is like it: 'Love your neighbour as yourself.' While people tend to follow the Ten Commandments in the Old Testament, the one which is most important is the commandment pertaining to love. If we adhere to that commandment, then it will not be difficult to obey the others.

The Ten Commandments represent the law given by the Creator of all men to his people by way of Moses. I am sure that Moses had such a love for God that he was called a friend of God. Nothing could separate him from the love of his Creator, and as a true friend he did all that God wanted him to do.

True friendship is priceless. We soon learn who our true friends really are, and, as the old saying goes, 'A friend in need is a friend indeed.' During various experiences in my own life, I have come to know who my true and loyal friends really are, and it is wonderful to know that you have someone on whom you can rely in times of need and to whom you can go for help with any problems.

I often hear patients say that during their deepest troubles their closest friends instinctively know exactly what to do or say to comfort them. Alfred Vogel and I had that kind of close friendship. We instinctively knew what the other was thinking or doing. I also know I can go to my great friend in Holland, Dr Hans Moolenburgh, with any problem I have. I might not speak to him regularly, but I know we can open our hearts to each other in times of need. This kind of friendship is based on love, and it can offer us peace in this sometimes hard and cold world in which we live.

The older I become, the more I worry that people today don't understand the meaning of real friendship. As we have seen in the previous chapter on loneliness, people are so busy these days that when something goes wrong and they need a friend in whom to confide, they often find that they are alone. I am also concerned that people are becoming more and more selfish. We need to take time to reflect on our lives and on our actions. If we have lost contact with friends who used to be important to us, we should ask ourselves whether this is the result of our own selfish actions. Have we been a good friend to those who needed us? Have we truly cared for those who are suffering? We need to remember that by helping others we also help ourselves – and it is this that gives our lives meaning.

The other day I gave a lecture, the proceeds of which were being donated to a particular hospice. Those who attended had a great love for the patients there, most of whom were nearing death. The enormous amount of money we raised to help keep this hospice running really touched my heart and restored my faith in humanity.

Nobel Prize winner Linus Pauling and I lectured together in several places throughout the world. At the age of 67, he had done a great deal to benefit the scientific world and felt he had accomplished everything he had set out to achieve in his career. Now he wanted to turn his attention to helping his fellow human beings, sharing his knowledge to help them improve their health, which he then proceeded to do from the age of 67 until he was 92. From his example we can learn that it is never too late to use our capabilities and the strength that God has given us in the use of humanity.

Those who think of me as a friend usually call me by my Christian name, Jan. This was the case not so long ago when an elderly lady passed me a large cheque for a charity on behalf of which I gave a lecture. She said that I had helped her 27 years ago, and she has had no problems since then. In handing me the cheque, she said that it was all the money she had, but she wanted me to give it to the less privileged. She was putting the needs of others before her own, and this demonstration of love towards her fellow human beings offered me great hope.

A Greek homoeopath, Anastasia, works with me in my Edinburgh clinic and devotes much of her time to treating emotional problems, including loneliness. Although I am a homoeopathic graduate myself, when patients consult me with these kinds of problems, I frequently ask her what she would prescribe for this or for that in order to make sure that I have not overlooked anything,

An elderly lady came to me the other day and said, 'I wish I had a few friends. I am so lonely and so unaccepted by others.' I asked Anastasia what she would give this lady besides the *Ignatia* I had prescribed. As we have already seen, *Ignatia* is an excellent remedy in times of sadness when you are coping with the loss of a loved one, as this particular lady was. When I told Anastasia this lady's life story, she asked me to try *Aurum*. What an amazing transformation came over that lady. She started to live again and later said, 'I feel happier now. The cold heart that I used to have is now surrounded by warmth. I love people again because of the new life that has been given to me.'

The happiness we feel due to the realisation that we have true friends is beneficial to the pancreas. It will begin to function better, and the secretion of digestive enzymes, and consequently the digestion, will improve. The inner secretions are stimulated with more production of insulin. There are many foods that can also help us achieve this happiness.

Happiness also begets friendship, as in order to be a good friend we need to have a positive attitude to life. This can be difficult when we are run down or suffering from some kind of ailment, and so we need to take care of our health. Many of us take good health for granted, but as Alfred Vogel said many times, 'Life is like good garden soil. It brings forth nothing if we do not sow and water and care for it.' One of the most important things we can do to protect our health is to get a good night's sleep. The sense of well-being one gets from a peaceful sleep, which is actually one of our best friends, makes us feel that we can conquer the world. Even if we have to work hard, as long as we can enjoy a restful sleep, then all our glands will benefit. The lymphatic system, which only works while we are asleep, does a wonderful job in cleansing our blood, and by morning we will appreciate what a great friend we have in nature. But it all needs careful attention. We cannot play around with our health, and when I see young people perhaps only getting three or four hours' sleep, I become worried.

When you feel miserable and you waken up in the morning with the bleak thought that you have no friends, life can lose its meaning. As I always say, negative will not look for positive, positive will look for negative, and then our health will be restored. But we have to take responsibility for ourselves. Leading a miserable life can be avoided. There is a way out. We just need to look a bit deeper to see what lies below the surface.

I remember a neighbour who was miserable, and yet I could see through her intricate needlework and the pride she took in her garden that there was more to her than met the eye. So I started to talk to her, and she ended up becoming one of our best friends. When we really got to know her, we discovered she had a good and loving heart. We just needed to look that little bit further. It is worth making that effort when the end result is a true friendship that enriches our lives.

Emotional healing is based on love and friendship. I read an article in which Thomas Baldwin talked about his meeting with Jean Vanier, founder of the worldwide L'Arche community for people with learning disabilities. Not only was it a lovely article but it also carried a very powerful message. I discovered that people with disabilities are crying out not for people to do things for them but for friendship. I agree wholeheartedly with L'Arche that real friendship is based on unconditional, unquestioning love – loving each other as we love ourselves. This is something from which everyone in the world can benefit.

When we really love someone, we would often rather be in pain ourselves than see them suffer, and our natural instinct is to offer them comfort. But sometimes even those closest to us can find it difficult to accept help; sometimes it is impossible to get through to them. In such cases, I have often used the following piece of poetry, which has been of great help to many people.

Most of us are acquainted with the quote, 'Laugh, and the world laughs with you; weep and you weep alone.' These are actually the first two lines of 'Solitude', a poem written by Ella Wheeler Wilcox in 1883 in which she describes the word so well. To those who are not aware of this poignant poem, I thought I would give you the opportunity to read it here:

Laugh, and the world laughs with you;
Weep, and you weep alone.
For the sad old earth must borrow its mirth,
But has trouble enough of its own.
Sing, and the hills will answer;
Sigh, it is lost on the air.
The echoes bound to a joyful sound,
But shrink from voicing care.

Rejoice, and men will seek you;
Grieve, and they turn and go.
They want full measure of all your pleasure,
But they do not need your woe.
Be glad, and your friends are many;
Be sad, and you lose them all.
There are none to decline your nectared wine,
But alone you must drink life's gall.

Feast, and your halls are crowded;
Fast, and the world goes by.
Succeed and give, and it helps you live,
But no man can help you die.
There is room in the halls of pleasure
For a long and lordly train,
But one by one we must all file on
Through the narrow aisles of pain.

This poem helps people to break through the negative thoughts that consume them and realise the true value of friends who are trying to cheer them up and help them through troubled times.

Didn't Mark Twain say, 'The best way to cheer yourself up is to try to cheer somebody else up'? Let's remember the true value of friendship, which can be one of our most powerful remedies when tackling emotional problems.

Keeping our emotions in balance is not always easy in this demanding world in which we live. However, we can learn to use our emotions as radars that quickly pick up when things are going wrong. Addressing these emotions as they arise will help keep us on track physically, mentally and spiritually.

Negative emotions will always creep into our lives, but when dealt with properly they are harmless. Always acknowledge them, preferably out loud. For example, say, 'I feel very sad because my best friend has chosen to ignore me.' Then take a philosophical view and say, 'But that is her choice, and I wish her only well. Now I must move on.' In doing this, you are transmuting a loss into a healing energy, and it won't start to fester and cause problems. This, of course, is dealing with such matters at a basic level. Deep-seated emotional pain and hurt will need more work to be released, but rest assured it can be.

Top scientists around the world are making great progress in the study of psychoneuroimmunology, the scientific study of the mind–body connection. I am always in favour of scientific study and innovation, but equally I respect the quiet power of the great healer, Mother Nature. I always like to remind people that the body has an innate intelligence that is always trying to help with healing, and I ask that it be listened to very carefully. Sometimes we need to stop seeking more information, just for a while, and be still and listen. We can learn a lot that way, too.

Index

abdominal pain 94, 96

acupuncture 39, 50, 57, 97–9,
    155, 160, 173
    depression and 81, 90, 92,
      99
    and drug addiction 113
    fear and 28, 32, 96
    jealousy and 66, 71
    in pregnancy 99
    relationship problems and
      99, 113, 115
    addiction withdrawal 19
    see also antidepressants
      tranquillisers; drug
      addiction

adrenal glands 13, 20

aggressiveness 14, 53

Agnus castus 162

Agrimony 35

alcohol abuse 14, 23, 53, 54,
    63, 92, 98, 105, 112, 114

allergies 168

anger 55
    and forgiveness 133
    harnessing 91
    and the liver 92–3
    repressed, and depression 92

anorexia nervosa 86, 139, 140,
    141

antidepressants 16–17, 77, 81
    and pregnancy 99
    side effects 16–17, 84

antispasmodics 22

anxiety 11
    alternative treatments 16–26,
      96, 159